MIKHAIL GORBACHEV, born in 1931, was General ~
tary of the Communist Party of the U
As head of state he introduced the r
country's foreign and internal polici
plete transformation of the Eastern Bl   ~~. ne was
awarded the Nobel Peace Prize in 1990, and in 1991 resigned
as Head of State. He became President of the Gorbachev
Foundation in 1992, and since 1993 he has been Chairman
of Green Cross International. He is the recipient of numerous
awards and the author of many publications including
Memoirs and *On My Country and the World*.

MANIFESTO FOR THE EARTH

ACTION NOW FOR PEACE, GLOBAL JUSTICE AND A SUSTAINABLE FUTURE

MIKHAIL GORBACHEV

CLAIRVIEW

Clairview Books
Hillside House, The Square
Forest Row, East Sussex
RH18 5ES

www.clairviewbooks.com

Published by Clairview 2006

Originally published in French in an earlier version under the title
Mon Manifeste pour la Terre by Ose savoir-Le Relié, Gordes, in 2002

Translated by Johanna Collis

A catalogue record for this book is available from the British Library

ISBN-10: 1 905570 02 3
ISBN-13: 978 1 905570 02 7

Cover by Andrew Morgan Design
Typeset by DP Photosetting, Aylesbury, Bucks.
Printed and bound by Cromwell Press Limited, Trowbridge, Wilts.

CONTENTS

Preface

Four years ago — when the French edition of this book was published — the world was slowly recovering from the shock of 9/11, the unprecedented atrocity that overshadowed all other events. However, it was still early in the new century. On the eve of the new millennium the international community had adopted many noble resolutions, as summarized in the UN Millennium Development Goals (MDGs). It seemed at the time that the deadline set for their implementation — 2015 — was far away, and that necessary progress could and would be achieved in time.

It is clear today that progress in the implementation of the MDGs is dangerously slow. Their critics say the MDGs are overambitious and that the targets set are unreachable. I totally disagree with that assessment. I believe they describe the minimum requirements for a decent human life. They express our commitment to a world where people have shelter, food and access to water and sanitation; where newborn babies and their mothers do not die from lack of basic medical care; and where gender inequality — that humiliating throwback to the past — has disappeared for good. If we cannot honour our commitment to these basic human necessities what future is there for our civilization — for our very humanity?

It seems less certain now that the 2015 deadline will be met, and I am astonished by the apparent lack of concern on the part of national governments, which are mainly responsible for meeting these challenges. This was once again demonstrated at the UN MDG Summit in September 2005. I am convinced that the road to finding solutions is blocked by the lack of political will, the paralysis of which – as underscored by the UN Secretary-General – can only be cured by using new ethical approaches. Once a moral stand is taken, with political decisions adopted and priorities set straight, the necessary financial resources will be made available.

I am convinced that the international community will not move ahead as long as the people allow their national governments to remain passive. Civil society, which in recent years has turned from an abstract notion into a real force, should take a more pro-active stand in solving the mounting problems. One recent example of this is the UK-based initiative, Make Poverty History.

As I state in this book, I believe the world is faced with three major challenges: those of security, poverty, and environmental degradation. It is obvious that development goals will not be achieved without stable peace and security in the world. Unfortunately, despite all the efforts made to ensure these conditions, a new fear has become omnipresent – the fear of terrorism. It is indispensable that the world community pulls together against terrorism, which cannot be justified by any political or moral arguments.

The second challenge involves combating world poverty. The fortunate 'haves' must stop looking with indifference at the sufferings of the 'have nots', who are half the world's population. Although official development assistance from the top twenty-two industrial countries to the least developed countries is now over $14 billion annually, this sum represents only a tiny percentage of these countries' gross national product.

The third is the ecological challenge. Sadly, recent events have offered more tragic proofs of the fragility of our world: the devastating tsunami in South-East Asia, the drama of New Orleans and the earthquake in northern Pakistan and India. One might even think Nature is taking 'revenge' against the arrogance of our civilization...

So, what can we do to make a difference? First of all, we need to scrutinize the structural factors inhibiting the transition to sustainable development, and we must better understand the mechanisms of globalization that are directing development on such a dangerous course. We need to bridge the gap between our consciousness and the challenges of our time. Consumerism and nationalism continue to pose a serious threat to achieving goals on sustainable development. A turnaround will not be possible unless states, communities and individuals are willing to reverse currently prevalent behavioural patterns. This turnaround must begin with changes in the human spirit, a reprioritization of our value system, including relations between people and the interrelationship between humanity and nature.

We need a Global Glasnost – openness, transparency, and public dialogue – on the part of nations, governments, and citizens today to build consensus around these challenges. And we need a policy of 'preventive engagement', so that military force ceases to be an option.

Mikhail Gorbachev
February 2006

THREE CHALLENGES FACING
OUR TIME

The beginning and the ending of a century rarely coincides with the calendar. Thus the nineteenth begins for me with the French Revolution and the twentieth with the First World War and the October Revolution. While the nineteenth created the basis for progress and democracy, the twentieth became the century of world wars and totalitarian ideologies. But it also stands for the liberation of many nations from colonialism and for the worldwide spread of the concept of human rights and ideas of social justice.

The twenty-first century, too, does not conform to the calendar. Its first portents were Perestroika and Chernobyl, but also 11 September 2001 (9/11). Why these events in particular? Perestroika brought an end to the arms race and the division of the world into two enemy camps and thus opened the way for genuine collaboration transcending national boundaries. Chernobyl was the terrible warning of dangers inherent in a technological civilization. And 9/11 showed up the horrifying consequences that can arise out of poverty and the loss of human values.

Whatever religious convictions we may have and whichever continent we inhabit, we cannot avoid three fundamental challenges facing us in the new century.

The first enjoins us to maintain world peace and direct every effort of the international community towards defusing so-called local conflicts. Participants in these are not only countries that possess chemical weapons but also those that have nuclear armaments or are about to develop nuclear striking power.

The second challenge concerns world poverty. The fortunate 'golden billion' must awaken to the sufferings of half the world's population who live on one or two dollars a day and frequently have no access to clean drinking water or any decent sanitation. In this age of the internet and globalization they should not be permitting millions of children to earn their living by hard labour instead of going to school.

The third challenge is ecological. We can see with the naked eye that climatic changes are taking place on the earth, that the number of natural disasters – hurricanes, storms, floods and droughts – is increasing, that many plant and animal species are dying out, that the polar ice caps are melting, and that the oceans are becoming increasingly polluted while the forests are being ever more rapidly destroyed. We have entered into serious conflict with our immediate environment, our natural surroundings.

These three global challenges facing humanity are closely interconnected on account of the fact that without unity in the world, without an end to wars and conflicts, it will be impossible to collaborate in tackling them as well as other fields involving efforts to save the planet.

If we do not combat poverty and overcome the gulf that separates the rich from the poor, the educated from the illiterate, we shall be powerless to deal with the fertile ground on which terrorism, fanaticism, crime and the misuse of drugs flourish. Ecological measures are meaningless if poverty is not tackled. How can you forbid a needy farmer in the Amazon Basin to cut down a section of rainforest and then till the soil thus laid bare? Can an impoverished country be expected to spend huge sums on ecologically clean industries?

Yet on the other hand, if we neglect ecology then all our efforts to create a fairer world will be doomed to failure. Our descendants will then find themselves for centuries if not millennia having to pay for our thoughtless addiction to wasting nature's resources. Indeed, life on earth might be entirely extinguished and become a passing episode in the history of our universe.

These three challenges concern not only governments and international organizations but each of us as individuals. The time has come for every inhabitant of the earth to think about what his or her individual contribution might be.

In a speech honouring the poet Alexander Pushkin which he gave in 1880, Fyodor Dostoevsky spoke about 'the world-embracing fellow-feeling of the Russian soul'. My book represents the outcome of many years of reflection by someone who once headed one of the world's two super-powers while never forgetting the humane traditions of Russian culture.

After the brutal warnings issued by Chernobyl and 9/11, let us hope that the twenty-first century will usher in a period of new thinking for humanity — a humanity that already knows deep down that it must live in a united world and that it is responsible for future generations.

HOW I BECAME 'GREEN'

Since leaving my post as President of the USSR and after the collapse of the Soviet Union, I am often asked why I have devoted my attention to ecology and taken on the leadership of a non-government organization, namely Green Cross International, which was founded in 1993.

We all want to make the best use of our abilities. And it seems to me that concerning myself with ecology in the widest sense will enable me to reach a kind of synthesis of my life, my life as a farmer, an intellectual, an economic functionary, a politician and finally as President of a state that encompassed one sixth of the earth's surface. For me environmental matters are inextricably bound up with peace, security and social justice.

I was born in the Stavropol region of the North Caucasus, one that had witnessed countless invasions and been a crossing point of many and varied cultures and civilizations. Its small territory has been home to three orthodox Christian confessions[1], to Islam and to around a dozen languages and indigenous cultures. Even today, in addition to Russians, the population includes Ukrainians, Greeks, Armenians and numerous peoples of the North Caucasus: Karachai, Circassians, Ossetians, Noghai, Chechens and others. So my home region schooled me early in tolerance and respect for other nationalities, languages, customs and religions.

Village life and that of my peasant family were closely bound up with nature – and thus also unavoidably with having to pull together to survive natural disasters and the effects of social injustices.

As a child I lived in poverty: in a traditional cabin with an earth floor. We slept on top of the Russian stove, and in winter a calf and in spring hens and ducks were kept under the same roof. In 1933, while I was still a child, Stavropol suffered a famine which was described in neighbouring Ukraine as 'planned starvation'. According to a number of historians it was artificially brought about by the government.[2] But more than anything else, collectivization had ruined agricultural production by destroying traditional peasant life and banishing the best farmers, the kulaks, to Siberia. In that terrible year nearly half the population of my native village, Privolnoye, starved to death, including two sisters and one brother of my father.

Another trial followed the famine: the Stalinist purges. Both my grandfathers were arrested on trumped-up charges, but fortunately they survived. But my wife Raissa's grandfather was shot and not rehabilitated until 1988.

Then, in 1941, a terrible tragedy struck the Soviet people: the attack by Hitler's Germany. My father was sent to the front while together with the rest of the family my mother and I, still only a young boy, lived through the German occupation, the hunger, the constant worry about my father (once we even received notification of his death, which later proved to be a mistake) and depressing concern for the fate of our country.

What is my strongest memory of those horrible years? There was that first winter of the war which was exceptionally cold, as though nature were trying to resist the invaders.

Then there were the hunger and poverty. The farmers had to hand over almost the whole of the harvest for the army and the armament production workers. There were no supplies even for our simplest daily needs. We reverted to a pre-industrial existence resembling the world 'after the catastrophe' as seen in Philip K. Dick's science fiction novel or as depicted in Tatyana Tolstoy's novel *Kys*. We sowed hemp and sheared sheep; grandmothers fetched their old spinning wheels and looms down from the attic; we even made our own footwear from cowhide, soaking the soles in Masut. Salt came from the salt lake 50 kilometres away; we learnt to use soda to make soap; we struck sparks with flint or manufactured matches from explosives we scraped out of unexploded shells.

Despite all this it was the following episode more than anything else which forever shaped my abhorrence of war. In late February or early March 1943, just as the snow was beginning to melt, I set off with a few other lads to hunt for 'trophies' in the undergrowth between Privolnoye and the neighbouring village of Belaya Glina. We happened on the remains of a group of our soldiers who had fallen in battle:

decomposing bodies in shreds of uniform, half devoured by wild animals, skulls in rusty helmets, bleached bones of arms and hands still clutching rifles, empty eye-sockets staring at us. This face of war, this image, so surrealistic in its realism, will remain in my memory forever. Whenever I hear of some new conflict or yet another act of terrorism I think of those soldiers as I listen to matter-of-fact reports about casualty numbers.

There is also another ghastly image that will never leave me. On my way to university in Moscow some years after the war I had to change trains in several towns where the most brutal battles had taken place: Stalingrad, Rostov, Charkov, Voronezh, Orel, Kursk. Endless kilometres of ruins . . . This, too, was the face of war.

Although my village had to struggle with cold, hunger and primitive levels of subsistence, the extent of our suffering was far less than that of the country as a whole: the occupation of a part of the USSR, the huge mortality of soldiers and officers, including some of my relations. What kept us alive was our belief in victory and the hope that life after the war would improve for the members of our *kolkhoz* (collective farm).

However, our life bore no resemblance to that depicted in post-war official propaganda. Books and films praising Soviet peasantry were produced showing *kolkhoz* members labouring like heroes and being rewarded by prosperity and plenty of fun in their free time. But our life was anything but full of fun.

At the age of 15 I began to help my father driving the combine harvester. It was crushing work, but all the members of the *kolkhoz* worked hard although they were not rewarded with money but only with measly 'payments in kind', i.e. farm produce. *Kolkhoz* families could only survive with the help of their private patches of land, and even from these they had to hand over a portion of their harvest to the state. And they had to part with a specific amount of milk, butter and meat even if they had no livestock. And fruit trees were taxed although they did not bear fruit every year.

In 1861 Tsar Alexander II liberated the Russian peasantry from serfdom although without interfering with the agricultural riches of the large landowners. The socialist utopia, for which millions of peasants had fought during the Revolution because it promised them land, turned under Stalin into a new form of serfdom. Now the peasants had become serfs of the state and were even prevented from migrating to the towns. The authorities refused them internal passes, and without such a document they could obtain neither work nor residence permits outside their own village. I soon began to realize – albeit only in broad outline – that Soviet peasants were the victims of social injustice. But I believed that their sacrifice would be short-lived and that a bright future would soon materialize.

During those post-war years I also became aware of the power of nature. For my granddaughters today, as for the majority of town-bred children, nature is a beautiful though abstract world: *trees* and *flowers* grow in woods and parks, and *birds* sing there. But if you ask them to name a simple wild flower or a warbling bird they cannot do so. Of course they have read Ivan Turgenev's *Sportsman's Sketches* but doubtless they skipped his impressive descriptions of the Russian countryside for they have never seen a single one of the many plants and animals he mentions. On the other hand, having been immersed in nature from childhood, I found those descriptions perfectly familiar: especially the enchanting world of the steppe with its endless distances where corn-crakes sing in the ripening wheat at sunset, where soft breezes murmur and a myriad of stars shine in the sky at night. At difficult times in my life Nature has always offered me refuge. For me it is not 'environment' or a 'place of leisure and relaxation' but a temple in which I experience feelings that are almost religious.

The natural disasters visited on our country in the post-war years showed me how dependent we are on nature. In 1946 almost the whole of the harvest in our region, and indeed in nearly all grain-growing areas, was ruined by drought. Countless hungry people descended on us from Stalingrad and other towns in the hope of exchanging anything they had for bread. The same scenes were repeated in 1947. And 1948 also began dramatically. For three days the whole of the North Caucasus was enveloped in dust storms so thick that you couldn't recognize a person standing five metres away from you. After the storms my father took me with him to look at our fields. The crops were crushed, flattened and buried under a layer of dust. My father was a reserved man who never raised his voice either at us children or at his wife, and in this situation, too, he did not weep or shout. But I saw the despair in his face. And then, a few days later, it rained, the crop perked up and recovered, and in the autumn we brought in a bumper harvest.

That was my first object lesson, which has to be seen against the background of the official doctrine of the time. Pinned up in every classroom was a maxim formulated by the famous agronomist Ivan Michurin who had succeeded in increasing the yield of apple trees by crossing various varieties: 'We cannot expect any gifts from nature – it is up to us to take possession of whatever it offers!' Several years later, when I returned from Moscow University to work in my native region, I soon realized what this formulation really meant.

Under Soviet conditions party leaders were first and foremost economic functionaries. So in the fertile region of Stavropol my efforts were focussed mainly on agriculture. This was a matter of rescuing the harvest in periods of drought, rescuing the cattle that were to be sent to Moscow, rescuing the soil which had become depleted through exploitation, and closing down the mines where gravel was won because this involved dynamiting the most beautiful hills of the North Caucasus. It was probably during that period that I swore to myself to devote all my power to change this situation one day. Little did I know how soon I would find myself in a position to do just that.

The higher I rose on the career ladder the more I saw before me the picture of the economic, social and ecological crisis for which the Soviet Union was heading. As we know, all information about the true state of the country was kept secret, and I only gained some access to it in 1970 when I had become a delegate to the Supreme Soviet of the USSR and a member of the Committee for the Conservation of the Environment. Not until I became General Secretary of the Communist Party did I become fully aware of all the details.

No care was being given to the earth, the fount of our existence; it was exhausted and laid waste. The state gave precedence to heavy industry which worked mainly for all aspects of armaments manufacture, and to the mining of our mineral wealth the sale of which was financing the arms race. Millions of hectares had been expropriated for military exercises. The construction of gigantic dams and the resulting artificial lakes needed for hydroelectric power stations had not only ruined the rich stocks of fish (in a country that had once been famous the world over for its fish delicacies) but also caused 14 million hectares of the most fertile land to be flooded. Further dozens of millions of hectares had been designated border areas. Primitive land improvement techniques had ruined huge once fertile territories. The careless application of pesticides had polluted fields, rivers and lakes and irreparably damaged flora and fauna. Especially affected was the far North where barbaric methods of oil and gas extraction had devastated parts of the tundra, the natural habitat of indigenous tribes. In the far East and Siberia incalculably valuable forest regions had been deforested. Then there is the Aral Sea which has lost 50 per cent of its surface area in the last 40 years. For decades the winds have been distributing across thousands of kilometres the salty dust mingled with pesticides which has formed on its dried up bed. This dust travels as far afield as Belarus and Afghanistan, destroying vegetation there. The basin of the Volga, the great Russian river along whose banks half the population of the Russian Federation lives, is also polluted. And in regions such as Chelyabinsk, where test areas for nuclear and chemical weapons had been fenced off, the population was not even warned of the dangers. We should not forget that in the 'closed'[3] town of Kyshtym not far from Chelyabinsk a chemical explosion took place in 1959 in a treatment basin for nuclear waste which caused serious poisoning of the population and the environment. This accident was kept secret for almost 30 years.

I was horrified. The lack of a public opinion permitted the leaders of the country to perpetrate unbelievable outrages without any mention appearing in media muzzled by censorship while functionaries of Party and State were rewarded with medals for their 'heroic deeds'!

In 1985 I was elected Chairman of the Communist Party which meant I became head of state of the USSR. By that time

I had already developed a number of ideas for reforming the country. Those ideas were supported by my firm conviction concisely summarized in the words: 'We cannot go on like this!'

I presented society with three aims: glasnost, perestroika and acceleration. An essential prerequisite for the reforms to which I gave the name of perestroika was glasnost or transparency, which gave people the possibility but also the right to speak the truth. How could reforms be put in train if one did not tell the truth about the actual situation, if people could not hear the truth about the past? The third aim meant that we must very quickly come to grips with the new technologies if we did not want to be pushed to the edge of the civilized world as electronics and computer technology forged ahead with their contribution to the process of globalization.

Freedom of expression electrified a society where problems had been building up for decades like the pressure in a boiler with its lid screwed shut. There were endless meetings, gatherings and discussions in the press and on television – society was bubbling over. And the first topic taken up by a newly awakened citizenship was that of ecology and the living conditions of the many millions of the Soviet population. In 90 towns of the Soviet Union, in fact in every large industrial centre, people were living in an environment of polluted air, water and soil. Women and children suffered the greatest ill health. Some protest meetings lasted for several days at a time. And we decided for ecological reasons to close 1,300 factories either forever or until they could be modernized. Even though several of them were producing essential goods we did not allow ourselves to be deflected from our decision. Under pressure from public opinion and the awakening civil society we also put a stop to the absurd 'pharaoh project' that planned to reverse the flow of Siberia's mighty rivers. It could have led to natural disasters in the whole of the Eurasian region.

The Chernobyl catastrophe which taught not only me but I hope the whole of humanity a lesson befell our country in April 1986, a year after I had been brought to power. According to the experts there was one chance in millions that the crew of the Chernobyl power station would make all seven mistakes at once that were needed for a catastrophe to happen. But happen it did, and the resulting explosion set the inside of the reactor on fire, causing it to blow its top so that considerable amounts of radioactive materials were flung into the atmosphere up to a height of one-and-a-half kilometres.

This was a new situation not only for our own scientists but for the world as a whole. Thousands of the Soviet Union's best experts – physicists, mathematicians, nuclear scientists, chemists – in Moscow, Kiev and Minsk were busy calculating every possible variation that might occur as the accident continued to worsen and suggesting ways of putting out the fire. Academician Velikhov and his colleagues warned the Politburo that the burning reactor might collapse. This would give rise to a thermonuclear reaction in which the critical mass would be ten times greater than that of the Hiroshima bomb. For understandable reasons we wanted to prevent panic breaking out, but in order to prevent an even greater disaster we deployed huge forces to extinguish the fire (which was continuing to send further radioactive particles into the atmosphere): many thousands of soldiers, fire-fighters and mineworkers continued to do their duty in the most difficult of conditions. Although each individual was relieved after only a few minutes, the amount of radiation to which they were exposed was so high that many suffered radiation damage and subsequently fell ill and died. After the fire was extinguished thousands of specialists continued to work for many months to decontaminate the Chernobyl area. These selfless individuals deserve our praise and our admiration for they knew that their life and health were in danger. They are the true heroes of our time!

I reject the accusations made against the Soviet government from time to time: that they did not give sufficient aid to the inhabitants of the affected areas. We did everything in our power. The fire was extinguished and the population evacuated, first within a radius of ten and then of 30 kilometres. Huge efforts were made to decontaminate residential areas, fields and meadows, and a 'sarcophagus' was placed over the damaged reactor in record time. In spite of the difficult economic situation of the country we spent dozens of billions of roubles on all this.

One unfortunate consequence of the splitting up of the Soviet Union was that neither the stage by stage evacuation of the affected populations nor the long-term measures being carried out were brought to a proper conclusion. Paradoxically, the treaty between the presidents of the three republics at Byeloveshskaya Pushcha[4] meant not only that the historical community of these three Soviet nations with their economic, political and human links was dissolved but also that each of the now independent states – Russia, Ukraine and Belarus – has been left with 'its own' Chernobyl problem. Belarus has suffered particularly as a result because 70 per cent of the radioactive fallout fell on its territory. Two million White Russians, one fifth of the population, still live on contaminated ground.

Chernobyl turned me into a different person, so what lessons have I learnt from the greatest technological calamity in human history?

Firstly, Chernobyl became a decisive test for the new policy of glasnost. Whatever may have been written about the matter, the following is the truth about what really happened: My government colleagues and I decided on the very first day to publish all the details about the catastrophe as soon as they reached us. In addition we kept foreign governments, especially our immediate neighbours, informed about developments. Members of the government committee held press conferences in Moscow on 6 and 9 May. And finally a detailed and well-accepted report was presented to the International

Atomic Energy Agency in Vienna by a Soviet delegation led by academician V. Legassov, one of the chief constructors of Chernobyl's RBMK Reactor and a first class scientist who, plagued by his conscience, later committed suicide.

Secondly, my belief in the absolute reliability of technology was shattered. For 30 years we had been assured that 'the peaceful atom was no more dangerous than a samovar', to quote academician A. Alexandrov's telling phrase, and that a nuclear power station could be built in Red Square without any problems. We had regarded physicists as demigods who with the help of science would fulfil humanity's ancient dream of cheap and 'clean' energy. Suddenly, however, these demigods had become vulnerable and were seen to possess human weaknesses. Therefore I gained the new conviction that all technological processes which might have negative effects on the health and life of the population require supervision by society.

Thirdly, my time-scales changed radically. The half-life of Caesium 137, the radioactive isotope most damaging to health that escaped from the 'cauldron of Chernobyl', is 30 years which means that this element will still be poisoning foodstuffs and affecting the health of populations in the polluted areas for a long time to come. What right have we to burden our descendants with such a problem? Whom should they blame for the misdeeds of our time?

And fourthly, Chernobyl stiffened my resolve to establish new international contacts and demonstrate emphatically that we are a single humanity sharing a single planet. After all, the radioactive cloud had spread around the globe within a few days, and traces of radioactivity had been found thousands of kilometres distant from the location of the catastrophe.

I had been thinking about a new concept of international relations for years. The Cuban Missile Crisis in 1962 had already shown that opposition between the two superpowers must on no account be allowed to lead to a nuclear conflict. Yet despite the politics of détente in the 1970s and despite the Final Helsinki Declaration the mutual distrust between the two blocs was so great that arms proliferation continued. Both arsenals were repeatedly augmented and the 'Nuclear Club' kept on growing.

I first had an opportunity to put forward my idea of a 'new political thinking' in December 1984 when I led a delegation of the Supreme Soviet to London even before I became General Secretary. This idea was based on convictions which I had found were shared by like-minded scientists at a number of universities. After talks with Prime Minister Margaret Thatcher I addressed the British Parliament. In my speech I stressed that there could be no winners in a nuclear age, that the cold war could not serve as a basis on which to conduct international relations, and that we were prepared to embark on limiting our arms, especially nuclear weapons, according to the principle of parity with our western partners. That was when I made the statement that has remained my creed to this day: 'However we may differ, we inhabit the same planet. Europe is our common home. It is a house, not a theatre of war.'

Despite resistance from western political circles and from the conservative parts of the Soviet party and state apparatus, the idea of this new political thinking gradually gained momentum. After the first Soviet-American summits in Geneva and Reykjavik a further theoretically important step was the New Delhi Declaration which I signed in November 1986 with the Indian Prime Minister Rajiv Gandhi who was murdered four years later by a Tamil suicide bomber, a woman. This declaration gave expression to several ideas which I considered essential for people in the twenty-first century. Among other points, we stressed that human life was of the highest value, that relinquishing violence was the highest priority in the co-existence of individuals and of nations, and that the 'balance of terror' would have to be replaced by a global security system.

Only a few years after I took up my position as head of state the political climate of the world had completely changed. Here are some of the milestones in those eventful years:

— A conference of the Organization for Security and Co-operation in Europe (OSCE) in Vienna in 1989. This culminated in the signing of an exceedingly important document which gave a new impulse to the talks on conventional disarmament in Europe. The document also contributed to strengthening the co-operation between all European countries and the role of human rights in the whole continent.

— The first Soviet-American treaty of 1987 on the destruction of land-based short and middle distance nuclear rockets which served as a prologue for the ratification of the START 1 and the START 2 Agreements[5] and led to the complete destruction of chemical weapons arsenals.

— The departure of Soviet troops from Afghanistan in late 1988 and early 1989.

— The departure of Soviet troops from eastern Europe, the dissolution of the Warsaw Pact, the introduction of multi-party systems and the transition to democratic government in all the countries of the eastern bloc during 1989 and 1990.

— The fall of the Berlin Wall and the re-unification of Germany.

In 1990 my endeavours to create a new system of international relations on the basis of peace, the recognition of universal human rights and without any ideological pressure were marked by the award of the Nobel Peace Prize.

My internal policies were guided by the same principles. The fundamental changes that took place during my years in government were: renunciation by the Communist Party of its monopoly on power and the introduction of a multi-party system; free elections; renunciation of centralism in relations with the Soviet Republics; renunciation of the use of force against nationalist movements; press freedom; religious freedom; economic reforms with the aim of a gradual transition to a market economy; unilateral reduction of the armed forces and the conversion of numerous armaments factories. From a totalitarian state in which every form of dissidence was punished, in which religious believers could not follow careers, in which every printed word was subject to Party censorship and thousands of books by contemporary writers and philosophers were stored in 'special archives',[6] the transition was made to a free society. Unfortunately perestroika did not succeed in improving the material living standard of Soviet citizens. But the reforms did make them free human beings who held the future in their own hands.

I shall not dwell here on the circumstances of my final year in office since they are well known, namely the putsch and the subsequent collapse of the Soviet Union which I had hoped to prevent so as to build a genuine federation with a common economic system.

Despite the disappointment I felt after my resignation in 1991 because of Boris Yeltsin's duplicity in sabotaging the signing of a new union treaty of sovereign republics[7] I relinquished the leadership with confidence. It seemed to me that the new thinking which had followed on from the cold war, and the multi-polarity that had taken the place of the two spheres of influence of the superpowers, had opened up new prospects for international co-operation, for example for a changed role of the United Nations, or for a joint struggle against poverty and international crime and for a healthy environment.

As I departed from my post as President simultaneously with the disappearance of the Soviet Union I decided to devote my future to my country and to humanity. Together with a number of my closest collaborators I set up the Gorbachev Foundation in order to develop further the idea of the new thinking and the idea of a new humanitarian civilization for the twenty-first century. I hoped that respected politicians and those working in the cultural sphere in every country would be attracted to join in the project.

The Earth Summit in Rio de Janeiro in 1992 gave me additional encouragement to return to a set of questions which, as I have said, had moved me deeply since my childhood, namely to save and conserve the environment – within the framework of a sustainable development based on social, moral and intellectual ideas. It seemed to me that this would be the best way of harmonizing my philosophical interests, my love for our earth and nature, my political experience and my moral authority. Above all I am convinced that this is the most urgent task facing humanity today.

THE GLOBAL CRISIS

I look back over the past decade with a <u>mixture of disquiet</u> <u>and disappointment.</u> The end of the cold war, symbolized by the fall of the Berlin Wall, had seemed to give cause for hope. It appeared that the world community, now free of nuclear threat and the shackles of ideological antagonism, would end the arms race and embark on a path of sustainable development; that it would take up the struggle against poverty and the catastrophic pollution of the environment, and that it could broaden the character of globalization to include concepts such as 'human rights' and 'personal freedom'.

These hopes were supported by a series of summit meetings during the 1990s, beginning with the <u>Rio Earth Summit</u> <u>in 1992.</u>

Perhaps because of my close contacts with a number of European statesmen, especially François Mitterrand, President of France (now deceased), I myself hoped that Europe would play a special part in the journey towards a new world order, not least because the ancient and dynamic European civilization had given birth to the original democracy — the Republic of Athens.

The history of Europe is unique. Over two-and-a-half thousand years it has undergone periods of expansion and of decline, of bloody internal conflict and war, of conquest and invasion. It has developed arts, sciences and technologies, given birth to nations and founded states. Europeans have learned the difficult art of living together while at the same time maintaining independence. Today this rare destiny and skill is more valuable than ever before.

In addition, Europe recreated itself on other continents and in doing so often tried to create a world in its own image. It built up dozens of new societies and states each of which carried on European traditions in its own way. It gave the world a sense of inner unity such as is essential for the new millennium.

The fall of the Iron Curtain brought about the disappearance of fatal antagonisms in the centre of Europe so that the continent was given a unique opportunity to build up pan-European structures. For the first time it might have been possible to realize the idea of a greater Europe stretching from the Atlantic to the Pacific with the inclusion of Russia of which General de Gaulle and later François Mitterand and I myself had dreamt – a Europe that has overcome its profound internal divisions; a Europe standing on the solid ground of shared values and ideals; a Europe capable of looking after itself while at the same time helping others; a Europe that can play a leading part in creating a global community; a Europe that could become a guarantor of globalization with a human face; and finally a Europe capable of resisting effectively the model of a unipolar world which the United States of America wanted to impose on humanity.

Unfortunately the opportunities on offer after the end of the cold war were for the most part not taken up. Humanity lagged disastrously behind the constantly accelerating rhythm of time. Exultation about the death of Communism continued for too long so that people ceased to notice the complexity of the world with its problems and contradictions. They forgot poverty and backwardness while the unstoppable problems of ecology were relegated to the outer edges of social awareness. In short, in place of a new world order we have ended up with a new 'world disorder' in which many countries, instead of tackling the global questions of human survival, have begun to cheat on one another in order to gain advantages for themselves to the detriment of others. As the American futurologist Alvin Toffler put it, we are already in the midst of an epoch of collision with the future.

The event of 9/11 showed the idea of a unipolar world to be utterly untenable and made it obvious that even the mightiest land on earth, the USA, is vulnerable and unable to cope on its own with the threat of international terrorism directed against it. I believe that this monstrous event marked the tragic downfall of the philosophy that had come to the fore after the end of the cold war and the collapse of the Soviet Union. But it also characterizes a new beginning which calls on people to unite in order to solve the global problems we all face.

So what conclusions can we draw from the period between the end of the cold war and the 9/11 attacks?

The political crisis

Despite the Russo-American agreement on the mutual reduction of nuclear arms signed by Presidents Bush and Putin in May 2002[8] – which of course I welcome – the past decade has shown that the end of the cold war in no way heralds the beginning of peaceful times. On the contrary, we have witnessed bloody conflicts in Europe, Asia and Africa: tension and terror in Israel and Palestine, three wars on the territory of the former Yugoslavia, two wars in Chechnya, ethnic conflict in Indonesia, an explosive situation in Kashmir, the crisis in the Persian Gulf, genocide in Rwanda, the war and international terrorism in Afghanistan – to name only the most obvious.

I shall analyse one of these situations, the one in Yugoslavia, because it reflects the fatal tendencies inherent in today's world order. One of these consists in the fact that some countries are endeavouring to create order by using force while pleading 'humanitarian motivations' and are meeting with scarcely any resistance from the international community. It was in accordance with this principle that the military actions against Yugoslavia were initiated because of the situation in Kosovo. As Russians know from bitter experience, in civil war no one is good or evil, saint or criminal, righteous person or sinner. People are only human, meeting under brutal circumstances and all too often losing their dignity. It would have been our duty to save them from this and prevent the commission of irreparable damage. Instead the most modern of weapons were deployed in a Europe that had known no war for half a century.

Having inflamed Serbian nationalism and bloody conflicts for ten years in the former Yugoslavia, Slobodan Milošević is now in the dock of the International Court of Justice in The Hague. But what about the leaders of the Albanian separatists and those who commanded the bombardment of the Serbian civilian population? Despite the presence of an international peacekeeping force Kosovo remains a time-bomb for it was Serbs and all other minorities who had to flee the region after the western intervention, and no longer the Albanians.

The Times newspaper has estimated a cost to NATO of a billion dollars per day for the war against Yugoslavia, a war – I hasten to emphasize – that could have been avoided. Would it not have been more sensible and more humane to use those funds for the struggle against poverty, unemployment, drug misuse and Aids in the developing countries and those of the former Yugoslavia?

There was another aspect, an ecological one, to the intervention by NATO. Although it had been known since Operation Desert Storm in Iraq that the use of depleted uranium resulted in radiation damage – as shown by the many illnesses contracted by the civilian population of Iraq as well as American and other western troops involved – these weapons were once again employed in Yugoslavia. Oil refineries and also petro-chemical and pharmaceutical plants were hit by NATO's bombardments. Who is now responsible for alleviating the damage done to the health of the Yugoslav and neighbouring populations?

I fear that other countries can only learn one lesson from this tragedy: To avoid suffering the same fate as Yugoslavia, borderline countries will have to develop their own nuclear arms as quickly as possible while poorer ones will need arsenals of chemical and biological weapons. And this in turn means that the world will once again face new horrors and dangers.

The measures implemented by NATO demonstrated not only the weakness of international organizations but also the lack of proper foreign and defence policies within the European Union. They showed that so far Europe has no political muscle that can be taken seriously and that it is incapable of acting as an equal partner in dialogue with the United States. Eastward expansion of NATO will change nothing in this respect; it will merely create new lines of division within the European continent.

Having gone through the trauma of the Second World War and occupation by the Nazis as a child, I shall never forget that the humane, Christian Europe of the twentieth century was not only the scene of two world wars but also their cause.

A new division of Europe would only be an anachronism leading to new conflicts. A new Golden Curtain would not be a jot better than the former Iron one!

The economic crisis

The end of the cold war and the avalanche of growth in information technology and telecommunications have given globalization a tremendous boost. Since it is a direct consequence of these developments it is obviously an objective process which can be neither halted nor altered. It is positive in many ways for it increases the wealth created in the world, intensifies the interchange between states, nations, peoples, regions and continents, creates possibilities for joining forces in searching for solutions to humanity's main problems, and brings with it new prospects for development.

How we make use of these possibilities is another matter, for as we know the road to hell is paved with good intentions. The past decade brought unparalleled economic growth to the USA and general increases in the welfare of most western countries. In the year 2000 alone the Gross World Product increased by 4.7 per cent to 31,362 billion dollars. And the volume of international trade increased by 12 per cent, reaching 6,253 billion dollars in the same year. Daily movements of capital on the world's stock exchanges amount to 1,300 billion dollars.

Nevertheless, for humanity as a whole the same decade witnessed the growing inequality between South and North, between poverty and wealth. And as a consequence of globalization and the free market economy, which absorbs capital and 'brains' from around the world for the benefit of only a few rich and powerful states, the gap is widening fast. Only one generation ago the wealthiest 20 per cent of the world's population were 30 times richer than the poorest 20 per cent. Now the difference is exactly twice as great.

The actual figures sound even more shocking. One billion inhabitants of the most highly developed countries, the so-called 'golden billion', are rewarded with 60 per cent of the world's income, while 3.5 billion inhabitants in the under-developed states get only 20 per cent. About 1.2 billion people live on less than a dollar per day. You don't have to be a Marxist to comprehend the explosive nature of this situation.

The total lack of control in the world's markets promoted by the international financial institutions has brought about many economic and financial crises, for example those in the countries of South-East Asia and also in Argentina and Russia.

Russia has demonstrated to the world what happens when a state without firmly established democratic institutions and lacking traditional capitalism 'with a human face' plays at being 'the best in the class' in handling liberal economic practices. In less than a decade the Russian population has been robbed and driven into poverty three times. Life expectation and the birth rate are both in decline. At the same time a phenomenon unknown since the civil war has reappeared: child homelessness. Yet Russia entered the world market with a high industrial potential, a well-trained work-force and plentiful natural resources. And there are many far more vulnerable countries that have been forced into the process of globalization.

The social crisis

When the cold war ended I hoped that at least a part of the huge sums spent on the arms race by the developed countries would be applied to rooting out poverty in the world. And I assumed that countries founded on Christian values such as charity would not be able to watch in silence while 800 million people suffered hunger, while over a billion people lacked access to clean water, while the dwellings of 2 billion people had no power supply, and while 3 billion, i.e. half of humanity, had to do without even the most elementary amenities.

How can anyone continue to indulge in satisfying needs only awakened by advertising in the first place when almost half of the earth's population has to make do with one or two dollars a day? How can equality of opportunity be cited in connection with globalization when the United States possesses more computers than the whole of the rest of the world put together, or when Tokyo alone has as many telephone lines as the whole of Africa, or when 130 million children of elementary school age have no opportunity to go to school?

The situation in Africa is especially tragic. Over the past 25 years the income and consumption of an average African family have decreased by 20 per cent. Of the 36 million people in the world infected by the Aids virus, 23 million live in Africa. The high mortality rate caused by this disease is lowering the average life expectancy of the population who have no access to expensive medication. Medical prognoses reckon with a reduction from today's 59 years to 45 years in the near future. In Botswana it is already only 41 years!

Meanwhile the aid goals the developed countries set themselves 30 years ago are far from being achieved. Instead of the promised 0.7 per cent of their gross national product, member countries of the OECD[9] spend only 0.22 per cent on development projects, and the richest country in the world, the United States of America, just 0.15 per cent. Winston Churchill once defined the difference between a statesman and a politician: Politicians think only of the next election while statesmen think of the next generation. There appears to be a great shortage of statesmen in the world today and an excess of politicians. Short-term electioneering considerations on the part of the latter and the consumerism of the population at large combine to push aside even an elementary sense of justice.

Yet today's world is smaller and more 'transparent' than ever. Thanks to radio, television and now the internet as well, everyone can assess the living conditions in any country, from the poorest to the richest. This knowledge makes the sacrifice of the victims of this inequality even more unbearable – thus adding yet more fuel to an already explosive situation.

When globalization gains ground in cultures not yet affected by it, the result often undermines or even destroys traditional structures. And if this involves a worsening of living conditions for large sections of a population it can make people receptive to religious fundamentalism. This process is further enhanced by direct contact with cultures and views of life that differ from lifestyles to which a population is historically accustomed. We can observe the consequences in, for example, the Moslem world.

Islamic fundamentalism is now 'winning over' one country after another. Since the 'Islamic revolution' in Iran several Muslim countries have returned to the shariah. Indeed, this traditional code of religious law, which in many respects contradicts the principles of modern civilization and human rights, has been adopted for the first time ever by a number of African states as well, while the Taliban in Afghanistan exercised total terror in the whole country. And here is a further example: After the declaration of independence by the former autonomous republic of Chechnya the Russians were shocked to find the shariah being introduced there, involving such things as punishments being meted out in public places.

Bearing in mind that in the next quarter of a century the urban population of our planet will double to five billion, it is almost certain that there will be an increase not only of crime, drug abuse and violence but also of religious fundamentalism and finally terrorism. Numerous examples have shown that terrorism arises in moments of historical crisis out of radical ideas that spread among impoverished populations.

As a convinced social democrat I am also dismayed by the growing influence of ultra-right forces not only in France but also in other European countries. However, it was comforting to note that the 'political earthquake'[10] in France mobilized public opinion sufficiently to halt the advance of fascism. In Italy, millions are also worried about the radicalism of their right-wing rulers and in a number of regions this has already given rise to an increase in votes in favour of left of centre forces.

The increase of right-wing extremism cannot, however, be explained solely as a reaction of European society to immigration or the splintering of democratic forces. In fact, the matter is a great deal more complicated and involves a high degree of protest against economic and social inequality. Unemployment remains high and is even increasing in some instances, especially amongst the young, and up to now this has challenged democratic institutions and is calling into question their ability to solve social problems. Many people feel alienated by politicians and power structures and are looking for ways in which to express their protest. So it is becoming increasingly apparent that democratic systems are also affected by the general crisis.

The ecological crisis

After the disintegration of the Communist system the famous French oceanographer and ecologist Jacques Yves Cousteau declared that nature had been damaged most not by Communism but by the market economy in which every item has a price but not a value. Although I do not want to advocate a return to Communism – now an outdated utopia – I am inclined to agree with Cousteau.

The growing ecological crisis shows that a liberal economy functioning mainly according to the criteria of profitability and a return on capital is not capable of coping with the ecological challenge. Today's market place ignores something that will be of inestimable value to humanity a hundred years from now. How, indeed, can we set about measuring the beauty of a lake or of a snow-capped mountain peak by using the yardstick of the market? How can the profitability of 'useless' animals or insects be calculated?

Nevertheless, in 1997 biologists and economists calculated the cost of nature's gifts to us – clean air, clean water, fertile land – to amount to 33,000 billion dollars per year. Not that nature is waiting to be paid, but is it not so that our descendants will have to raise at least that sum in order to put right the polluted environment we are leaving them?

Increasing numbers of scientists are admitting that the earth will face a deadly threat if we fail to make decisive changes over the coming 30 to 40 years. Put more precisely, it is not the house so much as its population that is under threat. Ecologists tell one another the following joke: Two planets meet in space. One looks ill and complains of having contracted *homo sapiens.* The other, bursting with health, replies: 'Don't worry, my friend. I had the same illness, but it went away entirely of its own accord.'

I remember how shocked I was when I heard about the extent of the ecological deterioration occurring in the Soviet Union. Today millions of politicians, economists, business people and ordinary citizens are equally shocked. Yet despite the openness of western society, public awareness is obstinately refusing to listen to the warnings of ecologists, biologists, geographers and meteorologists. For if we were to take what they are saying really seriously, every one of us would have to make radical changes in our lifestyle and in all our values.

Experts consider that life on earth today is undergoing a crisis more serious than that which wiped out the dinosaurs 65 million years ago. It is estimated that there are 12.5 million species of plants and animals on the earth of which only 1.7 million have been scientifically catalogued. It is incomprehensible that of the species known to us alone, 12 per cent are facing extinction. Every year 30,000 known plant and animal species are lost. This does not refer to tigers, elephants or whales which benefit from the sympathy of adults and children alike and can at least perhaps be saved in zoos, but to countless millipedes, snails, birds and insects. In addition to millions of plants and other living creatures, one hectare of tropical rainforest also contains more tree species than occur in the whole of Europe from the Atlantic to the Ural Mountains. If Brazil continues to clear the forests of the Amazon Basin at the present rate, and if Indonesia continues to deforest Borneo and Sumatra, we shall have lost half the earth's biodiversity at the latest by the end of this century.

In her book on Chernobyl, the Belorussian writer Svetlana Alexiyevich quotes a man who was involved in the cleanup after the catastrophe. He was one of a group digging out layers of soil contaminated by the radioactive fallout and 'interring it in special coffins'. Of course someone who considers soil to be our 'bread-giver' will find it hard to come to terms with the thought of 'interring' it. But this man was especially surprised at the multitude of insects entirely unknown to him which he found living in that ground: 'Living layers of earth . . . with beetles, spiders, worms in them . . . I didn't know their names, I had no idea what they were called . . . They were just beetles and spiders. Ants. Large and small ones, yellow and black. So colourful. In a lyric poem I once read of animals being little tribes on their own account. I killed them by the dozen, by the hundred, by the thousand without even knowing their names. I destroyed their dwellings. Their secrets. I buried . . . and buried . . .'[11]

What right have we to decide whether these creatures should live or die in order to protect ourselves against the consequences of a technological catastrophe? What right have we to destroy them simply through our lifestyle which destroys their natural habitat? After all, as the American scientist Edward Wilson emphasizes, every species represents a library of information gathered over hundreds of thousands or even over millions of years.

Loss of biodiversity is only one aspect of the ecological crisis which our unrestrained lifestyle has visited on the earth. While the USA bargains over the conditions under which it will agree to sign up to the Kyoto Protocol[12] which is intended to reduce greenhouse gas emissions, scientists have already calculated that during the course of the present century the average temperature of the earth will rise by between 1.2 and 3.5 degrees Celsius. The consequences of climate change resulting from the greenhouse effect and the destruction of rainforests are that the polar ice caps and glaciers from the Alps to Kilimanjaro are melting while sea levels rise unremittingly, endangering many islands and coastal towns.

Increases in the temperature of the earth mean that polar bears and penguins, the Pacific salmon and complicated organisms like coral reefs will gradually disappear. Greater evaporation will dry up rivers, which will result in drinking water shortages and desertification. In the past decade the number of floods, hurricanes, tropical storms and other natural disasters has quadrupled in comparison with the 1960s. Four times more damage was done by natural disasters in 1998 than in the whole of the 1980s.

Climate change and the accompanying drought, starvation and natural disasters must be seen as serious threats to peace and world stability. The most dramatic effects will be in the countries and among populations where poverty is greatest, for these are situated in regions which are also politically the least stable. Every year already 25 million people are becoming ecological refugees. So what about the future?

Like the sorcerer's apprentice humanity is encountering more and more problems which, for example the arms race, are caused by technology itself, and also more and more technological catastrophes which are usually the result of human error and ecological nihilism. Our environment is being destroyed by acid rain, erosion and pollution of agricultural land and by heavy metals and chemicals that burden both soil and water. In addition there is the nuclear pollution of the Arctic and a number of other regions. None of us can forget Chernobyl, Bhopal, and foot-and-mouth disease in Europe, or the oil slicks along the coasts of Alaska and France after the *Exxon Valdez* and *Erika* accidents.

Shortages and destruction of natural resources are also the direct consequence of population growth. Over the last 25 years world population has increased by 2 billion to more than 6 billion. In a quarter of a century this will rise to 8 billion; in 2050 there will be 9 billion and by the end of the century 11 or 12 billion. How can we guarantee a suitable standard of living if we continue to use up natural resources and ruin our biosphere?

The greatest danger is likely to be the shortage of potable water. Even today water reserves in many countries are insufficient, especially in the Near East and northern Africa but also in China and India. Over one third of the world's population lives in countries where water shortages are the norm and where water use exceeds the renewal potential by 10 per cent. In a world where 30 to 40 per cent of food is produced on irrigated land and where droughts will be on the increase owing to global warming, water shortages are also likely to become disastrous for agriculture.

In addition to the plundering of water reserves and the soil, the intensive exploitation of fossil fuels that have taken millions of years to form will also unavoidably lead first to price increases and finally to their disappearance. Various estimates indicate that oil reserves will be used up in 50 years at the latest. Coal reserves are by no means exhausted as yet, for there is sufficient for a good many centuries to come, but burning coal leads to the production of greenhouse gases. There is also still plenty of uranium, but using nuclear energy on a large scale creates insoluble problems concerning the disposal of radioactive waste.

What kind of a world are we going to leave to our descendants? Will humanity be faced with an epoch of wars about water and other resources? Will population and production growth continue until all natural resources are exhausted and the industrial world comes to an end, as Lester Brown and other futurologists have predicted?

By nature I am an optimist and so I hope that humanity will come to its senses before these developments become irreversible. Nevertheless, a tremendous gap now separates us from the optimism of scientists who only a few decades ago believed firmly in the omnipotence of human reason!

In Russia the great scientist Konstantin Tsiolkovsky is regarded as the father of space travel because he discovered the principle of rocket propulsion. In 1925 he wrote in his philosophical work *Monism Vselennoi* ('Monism of the universe'): 'The earth's population can increase a thousandfold and still retain the greatest prosperity. If there were no limit to the amount of solar energy allocated to the earth it would be transformed into living matter . . . The human being will become the true ruler of the earth. He will remodel the continents, alter the composition of the air and make abundant use of the oceans. The climate will adjust itself to his wishes and requirements. The whole earth will be habitable and bear plentiful fruits . . . Future technology will overcome the gravitational pull of the earth thus making it possible to travel throughout the solar system. All its planets will be visited and explored. Imperfect worlds will be wiped out and replaced by others harbouring human populations. The sun will be surrounded by artificial dwellings for which planets and their satellites will supply the building materials. This will make way for a human population two billion times greater than that left behind on the earth . . . It is difficult to imagine the civilization of the future human being, his prosperity, his luxurious lifestyle, his insight into the universe, his enjoyment and his unclouded and unlimited happiness. No billionaire can possess anything like this today.'

These words, so characteristic of the enthusiasm about the unlimited possibilities of science which held sway in the first half of the twentieth century, now bring no more than a wistful smile to our lips. Human beings have certainly become the absolute rulers of the planet; they have inexorably exploited the resources of land and ocean; they have altered the composition of the atmosphere and the climate; and they have travelled through the solar system. But these transformations, which favoured a population increase and a rise in life expectancy beyond anything hitherto known in history, have not subjugated nature but plundered it.

For 200 years historians and archaeologists have been trying to decipher the script of the Easter Island people and discover why an ancient civilization that was still creating monumental works of art in the fifth century after Christ should have perished. The anthropologist Clive Ponting has one answer.[13] The reason why the 7,000 inhabitants of these tiny, isolated islands died out was connected with the destruction of the ecological balance, and especially the deforestation which they themselves perpetrated. Ponting concludes: 'The fate of the Easter Islands is a symbol for the overall population of the earth.'

Humanity now knows that space tourism is a privilege for billionaires and that this planet is our only home. People are aware that the earth with its resources and its biosphere is finite.

In the 1920s the great Russian scientist Vladimir Vernadsky laid the foundation for the science of the 'noosphere' which was later added to by the French philosopher Edouard Le Roy[14] and the palaeontologist Teilhard de Chardin. In his philosophical works, which have only recently been published,[15] Vernadsky expressed the opinion that the biosphere, reshaped by the human spirit, was entering a new phase because humanity – the crown of a long palaeontological evolution – had become a new biological force. This would transform life on earth and open up new energy sources and a process by which food could be directly synthesised. However, unlike Tsiolkovski and other Russian and western scientific utopians, Vernadsky warned – as early on as the 1930s – that absolute rulership of the planet by humans would be dangerous because this might threaten, for example, natural resources or biodiversity. He was highly critical of Communist ideology which he regarded as being responsible for famines and the death of huge numbers of people as well as for the economic failure of the system. He wanted the social role of science to be recognized, and sought to found an organization that would represent humanity's moral and religious ideals and guarantee a dignified life regardless of the unequal distribution of wealth.

The hour has come for all of us to shoulder responsibility for the fate of the earth and its future. We have changed it beyond recognition and it is now up to us to ensure that life on it will continue.

WHAT IS TO BE DONE?

Deisaku Ikeda, the well-known Japanese Buddhist, once told me the following Oriental parable:

Let us assume that each day the water lilies on a pond double the amount of the surface they cover. If the whole surface is covered on the thirtieth day, this must mean that on the twenty-ninth day half of it will still be visible. Someone looking at the pond on the twenty-ninth day might conclude that since half the surface is free of water lilies there is no cause for panic. But in fact only one day remains before the whole pond is overgrown!

Deisaku Ikeda concluded: Today's world with its demographic problems and excessive exploitation of natural resources and fossil fuels is now living through its twenty-ninth day, and it might find that on the thirtieth day it has no more reserves to call on.

Of course in the critical situation we have inflicted on the earth there are various scenarios that might apply, one of which could be as gloomy as that portrayed by Mitterand's former adviser, the businessman and intellectual Jacques Attali.[16] He foresaw a war of the rich West against the rest of the world and an increase in conflicts like those of Yugoslavia and the Near East in which nations would be split along ethnic or religious lines. In every megalopolis the rich would live in quarters fenced off like fortresses for protection against the anarchy and criminality of the poor. An upper class of highly qualified technocrats living in luxury would form while half of humanity, around four billion people, would be condemned to leading a roving existence in search of food. And, the author wrote, all this would come about despite a general acceptance of the ideas of fraternity and charity.

But the future cannot be predicted. None of the marvellous or terrible scenarios described by science fiction writers such as Yevgeni Samyatin or Isaac Asimov has actually come to pass. Yet the events of real life have certainly taken us by surprise. Who could have foreseen the fall of the Berlin Wall even one or two years before it happened? Or the dissolution of the Soviet Union? Who could have predicted 9/11? Yet these have been real turning points in world history.

But even if we cannot predict the future we should do everything in our power to prevent our planet's 'thirtieth day' becoming one of global catastrophe in which scenarios like that portrayed by Jacques Attali become reality. The question therefore is: What is to be done?

To a Russian intellectual this question might appear ironic, for in his day the Russian writer and democrat Nikolai Chernyshevski put the same question in his novel of the same name about the 'new men' – the revolutionaries. And Lenin, too, gave the title *What Is to be Done?* to one of his works. Poking fun at both, the Russian philosopher Vasily Rosanov, who did not approve of the Revolution, wrote early on in the twentieth century: 'What do you mean, what is to be done? Make jam in summer and drink tea in winter!'

Of course I do not claim to be any kind of a prophet; nor do I intend to make suggestions for a new social revolution. But neither do I feel that Rosanov's recipe of sitting hands-in-lap drinking tea will get us very far towards overcoming the global crisis we are facing. What we need is not a revolution but an evolution of the idea we harbour about ourselves and about how the world might be organized and what its new shape in the age of globalization might be.

Not only the majority of ecologists but also politicians acting under many different forms of state now agree that the earth is in need of sustainable development. International programmes aiming at this have been set up, and in many countries ministries or secretariats have been established to work on the problems of ecology and sustainable development. Yet although the concept is now firmly established within the language of officialdom there are many sections of the population that are still not familiar with it.

The idea of sustainable development was first formulated at the 1972 UN Conference on the Human Environment in Stockholm. The concept was later fleshed out in 1980 in the paper on a 'global strategy for the conservation of nature', published by the International Union for the Conservation of Nature, which discusses development that is driven not only by economic considerations but also by social and ecological imperatives. Consequently it is less a matter of quantity and more one of quality. Norwegian Prime Minister Gro Harlem Brundtland gave the best definition of this complicated and multi-facetted concept in a United Nations report in 1987. She spoke of 'development that satisfies the needs of the present time without jeopardizing the ability of future generations to satisfy their needs'.

At the Rio Environment Summit the idea of sustainable development was promoted to programme status by the Rio Declaration on the Environment and Development. Under the heading 'Agenda 21' a number of agreements on climate change, biodiversity, forest resources and desertification were also published together with various concrete though not legally binding suggestions.

Since then over ten years have passed during which numerous further international conferences have taken place. Also many measures have been firmed up at government, regional or local level and NGOs have been activated while ecological awareness has grown in many countries. Nevertheless these ten years have also shown that despite isolated successes humanity at large is falling seriously short of solving the pressing problems of its survival. The pace of environmental deterioration is not being held back by the comparatively hesitant measures being taken. I cannot forget what someone said during one of the conferences: 'Humanity resembles passengers on board the *Titanic* carrying chairs from a lower to a higher deck while the ship was sinking into the sea.'

On the other hand there is no point in merely reproaching our contemporaries. In all its history humanity has never faced tasks as complex as those we are encountering today. In the century of globalization the inhabitants of the earth must find ways of managing the complicated economic and social processes involving six, and soon eight billion people. Decision-making processes that do not involve conflict must be worked out, the delicate balance between differing national, ethnic, religious and cultural interests must be protected and the mentality of our consumer society transformed.

Criticism of globalization voiced in the developing countries and in some circles in western society is justified when the concern is directed at the way globalization tends to run hand in glove with the hegemonic aims of the USA and the West. But the phenomenon itself is actually far more complex. What does globalization mean in practice?

Past cultures rarely shut themselves off into a state of autarky. People moved about, conquered new territories, traded with others and went on journeys. We need only think of the Roman Empire, the great Silk Road, the travels of the Italian merchant Marco Polo and the Russian trader Afanassi Nikitin to China and India, the discovery of America, the colonial wars and the more recent empires. But in the twentieth century the two world wars became tragic forerunners of globalization which, for various reasons, has since then adopted an entirely new character in our time.

First of all the universal validity of certain important principles, especially that of human rights, has been recognized. And effective though still far from sufficient instruments for regulating international relations have been created: the United Nations, the Organization for Economic Co-operation and Development, the International Monetary Fund, the World Trade Organization, the World Bank, and many others.

Secondly antagonism between the hostile blocs and their satellite states ceased when the cold war ended, so that effective co-operation is now possible at all levels.

Thirdly a quantum leap has taken place in information technology. With the internet a medium has been created that allows people to do brisk business across all continents, to speculate on any stock exchange in the world without having to leave their house, to shop in any corner of the world, to communicate with one another and exchange information and experiences, and to receive an academic education or medical advice even in the most distant and isolated places.

The globalization of the economy and politics is also gaining ground rapidly because for the first time in its history humanity is faced in the twenty-first century with challenges that can only be tackled by concerted action. As I have already stated in the first chapter, the three most important challenges of the twenty-first century are closely interconnected and global in scale: the preservation of peace in the whole world, the struggle against poverty, and the protection of the environment. Armed conflict, poverty and environmental problems including the dwindling supply of raw materials were not caused by globalization, but the only way to deal with them now is to join forces. Not only trade but also organized crime and epidemics have no respect for borders.

To be sure, globalization is rightly criticized for being of use mainly to highly developed, industrialized countries. The new system of an open, borderless world has overtaken nations and states in varying stages of development. The countries best prepared for the demands of our time through having a modern infrastructure, a highly qualified population and progressive technologies were at an advantage from the beginning. The process of globalization has proved to be asymmetrical. The economically and politically dominant countries have protected their interests by developing double standards and withdrawing into a selective application of the principle of openness. Meanwhile the countries 'at the periphery' — where the majority of humanity lives — have had foisted on them the thankless task of supplying raw materials and cheap labour.

The countries of tropical Africa are in an exceptionally difficult situation and need to be reintegrated into the processes of the global economy as quickly as possible. The EU and the USA cannot avoid accepting that their internal agricultural subsidies are condemning African farmers and those in other developing countries to unmitigated misery. For example, if global market prices for cotton were not kept so low by subsidies in the developed countries, the number of poor people in Burkina Faso (where the average income is less than a dollar per day) would be halved within six years.[17] Something urgently needs to be done for African countries: debt release, better access to world markets, increase of direct investment from abroad, and of course increased aid. The international community must work out strategies as quickly as possible to bring economic equality to impoverished, vulnerable and marginalized countries, in the first place those of Africa.

Since globalization is still in its infancy there are many rules which are still unknown to us. Much of what is built up will depend on what we ourselves have the will to do. As inhabitants of the earth, we shall all have to work towards making globalization a model for sustainable development for the benefit of humanity as a whole, towards ensuring that global financial crises do not always knock 'the weakest', towards preventing multinational companies from becoming the main beneficiaries of globalization, and towards helping humanity to preserve its variety. I am especially keen that those who are strong do not isolate themselves from representatives of international civil societies, as happens at present at economic summit meetings, but instead enter into constructive dialogue with them. The split between those who are for and those who are against globalization, both in the rich North and the poor South, is rather like an automatic application of old ideas of class struggle to a new reality.

The first thing needed for the transformation of globalization into something that will benefit the whole world is a worldwide steering system or, as some are already suggesting, a world government. I would find this utopian, undemocratic and dangerous. It would be more advisable to make more effective use of existing authorities such as the UN, the International Monetary Fund, the World Bank or the World Trade Organization. These could be given greater powers to create a democratically organized, uniform world community to which all countries would belong as equal members. It would be extremely important to consider ecological and social factors when making international economic decisions. To regulate fair international trade there would need to be rules that strengthen individual economies and help eliminate poverty. And one would have to introduce effective mechanisms such as the Tobin Tax[18] for controlling financial markets and guaranteeing sustainable development.

Democracy will now have to prove that it can do more than merely provide a counterbalance to totalitarianism. This means that we must make it the pivotal principle of international relations. The reason for this is not only that it would guarantee the equal rights of all countries but also that democracy stands for openness and freedom of opinion and information. Without it, awkward truths would inevitably be suppressed, as was the case for many decades in the Soviet

Union. An authoritarian regime with its bureaucratic structure is easily bribed; it might grant permission for a project damaging to public health and then cover up ecologically or socially catastrophic consequences. One such example is China, where the construction of the gigantic Yangtze dam has led to the relocation of two million people and the flooding of towns, historical sites and agricultural land. Also in China, the fact that millions of its inhabitants were infected with the Aids virus was kept secret for years.

✓ International bodies must bring transparency into their decisions and the way they are executed. And above all it is time to think about a reform of the United Nations that would render its authority indisputable. When some states take it upon themselves to behave like cowboys in the Wild West – proceeding to carry out military or policing operations without a mandate, or not following resolutions passed by an overall majority – then it is clear that the United Nations Organization cannot continue to exist in its present form. For if it does, the door will be open for chaos and conflict in a world where all kinds of nationalisms are already coming into being in a way that resembles an allergic reaction to globalization, where archaic syndromes of ethnic and religious enmity are on the increase, and where equally archaic brutality bursts out as it did, for example, in the Rwanda genocide.

The United Nations Organization was founded after the Second World War, and to this day its structure reflects the circumstances that had arisen after the Allies' victory over Nazi Germany and imperialist Japan. It was a time when the world consisted of the victorious and the vanquished, and this is the only explanation as to why those two great and now democratic nations still have no permanent seat on the Security Council.

In my opinion the time has come to remove Article 53 on 'enemy states' from the Charter of the United Nations. In order to enhance the importance and influence of the Security Council and make it more democratic, I suggest that respected states like India, Italy, Indonesia, Canada, Poland, Brazil, Mexico and Egypt should become permanent members, even if initially they cannot exercise a veto. Finally I should like to mention an idea which means a great deal to me, for its realization might remedy the moral deficit of present-day politics. In all traditional societies the 'Elders' enjoy a high degree of respect and exercise great moral authority. Surely it would be a good thing to link a 'Council of Elders' with the United Nations to which recognized scientists and artists, Nobel laureates, bearers of high office in various religions and respected retired politicians from our 'global village' would belong? Today's politicians will not be able to avoid making politics more human.

Since ecological threats are becoming more acute and natural disasters as well as technically induced catastrophes are on the increase, I would also consider it advisable to grant power to the Security Council to act in these matters.

Although I am no friend of puffed-up bureaucratic structures, I did like the former French Prime Minister Lionel Jospin's suggestion to make the United Nations' programme for the environment the foundation of a fully-fledged world organization. This would make it possible to balance the influence of the international bodies that want to compel the developing countries to participate in a pure market economy. Numerous existing international conventions could be standardized and their function supervised. And the United Nations would be able to exert pressure on countries who kept putting off signing and ratifying international agreements, conventions and protocols on disarmament, climate change, biodiversity, desertification and water reserves.

Another idea which I have tirelessly supported is the creation of an international ecological court modelled on the Human Rights Tribunal in The Hague. This would on the one hand exercise arbitration functions and on the other would convict countries or private enterprises that damage the environment or the population. So far there is no way of punishing the guilty, especially when the whole of humanity is the victim. Who will set up sanctions against countries that have ratified the Kyoto Protocol but fail to fulfil their promise to reduce emissions responsible for the greenhouse effect by the year 2012? Who in the rich countries will make good the damage done to the environment of poor countries by these gas emissions?[19]

Regional organizations need enlarging as well. In my

opinion the European Union is of special significance because it embodies the unique model of a successful merger of countries which share a common value system while at the same time having rich cultural differences and not even a common language.

The countries of Central Europe have now joined this well-integrated, democratic western Europe. However, it will be important to remember eastern Europe as well and refrain from setting up new lines of division that could squeeze it into a Procrustean bed of preconditions that are too restrictive. The new Europe, which is feeling its way into the future as regards international integration, the social protection of its citizens, and ecology in the name of all humanity, must be built up from the East as well as from the West. And in this, Russia could have an important part to play.

Admittedly, neither general nor specifically concrete measures taken by governments and international organizations will succeed in coming to grips with the struggle against poverty, ending armed conflict, dealing with the results of war or protecting the environment if the mentality of the consumer society does not change. This mentality is advancing everywhere in tandem with globalization. It will have to be confronted, for it is corrupting people everywhere and bringing them into conflict with nature.

I remember a conversation I had with former Secretary of State George Schultz when visiting the USA a few months after resigning as President of the USSR. We talked all night, and I explained to him: 'You Americans want to impose your lifestyle on the whole world. But you use 44 per cent of the electricity produced worldwide. If other countries follow your example, all the earth's reserves will be used up in a few years.'

That was in 1992, and the situation has not improved since then. On the contrary, we now face the paradox of seeing almost a billion people going hungry while half of all Americans are overweight and suffering the consequences.

In recent decades the economy in industrial countries has been creating consumer demands rather than merely meeting them. It has been 'uncovering' subliminal needs, declaring that these must be met at all costs, and making sure that the consequent new branches of industry flourish and work to capacity. The economy has not merely grown; it has created a new quality of life and changed society. Furthermore, in all countries with liberal markets consumption has been declared the engine of economic development. In addition to being subjected to advertising, people are told emphatically that they are combating unemployment if they buy home-manufactured goods. So the concept of consumption is raised up to be more or less on a par with patriotism. However, we are now having to admit that consumer attitudes and excessive demands on nature are coming up against ecological, social and moral limitations.

The industrial nations will have to strike the difficult balance between their own economic interests and ecological imperatives. I support the suggestion which has already been made many times: that the costs of present and future damage to the environment must be included in the price of goods and services that have generated those costs. For example the price of electricity from nuclear reactors must include the future cost of dismantling the power stations which can only run for a few decades, and the cost of dealing with the resulting radioactive waste.

Reorientation of consumption after the introduction of realistic pricing for goods and services might lead to economic decline in some branches, but it would create new workplaces in others. New ecologically friendly industries, rapidly expanding recycling of industrial and household waste, and the development of nature reserves and the eco-tourism that would result from these would all be greatly labour-intensive. And there is also a shortage of carers in an ageing society, and of teachers, social workers and those who work in the spheres of the arts and entertainment.

Of course finance will be needed to pay for all these new work places. Part of the funds would have to come from the 'polluting industries' themselves (as in the case of industrial waste which it is not usually profitable to recycle). But for the most part it will be a matter of state and local budgets providing the means. We shall have to admit that our consumer society has outlived itself and that we must tighten our belts. If we do, our quality of life will improve and we will be living in harmony with our conscience instead of beyond our means. For this to happen, however, the turnaround in social awareness which is already perceptible will have to come fully into play.

In one of her interviews the well-known anthropologist Maritta von Bieberstein Koch-Weser recalled the centuries-long building of cathedrals during the Middle Ages. It took 500 years, for example, to build Cologne Cathedral. People paid taxes and humped building materials knowing that the cathedral would not be finished in their lifetime and that their distant descendants would be the first to pray in it. Applying this image to our present time would mean taking into consideration what will happen in the year 2500. This is the anthropologist's way of looking at the principle of sustainable development which is the exact opposite of the Latin saying: *Carpe diem!* [Seize the day!].

We shall have to create a new civilization and may be helped in this by the Native American philosophy handed down to us: 'We have not inherited the earth from our parents but borrowed it from our children.' We shall all have to change in a way that will let the verb 'to be' become more important than the verb 'to have'. It will be necessary for us at last to grasp the fact that we are not alone on the earth and are not here solely for our own sake, that human beings are not the rulers of nature but a part of it. This thought should become an immutable component of our moral principles.

Sceptics may accuse me of preaching a new utopia if they wish, but they should not forget that I have witnessed several generations of Soviet people working patiently with much suffering trying to build a Communist utopia. Perhaps the sceptics would like to charge me with trying to conjure up the 'new man' although all previous attempts to create such a being have emanated from totalitarian ideologies. I have not forgotten a sarcastic quotation from the memoirs of the great Russian singer Feodor Shalyapin: 'The unfortunate thing is that our Russian architects will not condescend to build a sensibly designed ordinary building for ordinary people. At all costs they have insisted on building a tower reaching up to the sky . . . But even that is not the most astonishing fact: Our Russian wise men have the disconcerting gift of being all-knowing. They can transform a hunchbacked cobbler into an Apollo of Belvedere and teach a hare how to strike a match; they know what will make hares happy and even what will make their descendants happy two hundred years from now.'

Are we, the proponents of sustainability, behaving in the same way?

Certainly not!

Unlike a totalitarian utopia, sustainable development is not a blueprint for a new world that cannot yet be clearly seen. Sustainability is a 'terrestrial project' aiming for the long-term survival of humanity on the earth despite its finite resources and its damaged ecosystems, a project arising out of a diagnosis of our problems founded not on compulsion but on international consensus. And one might say the same about the 'new man'. No one is calling for the forced re-education of our contemporaries after the manner of the Chinese cultural revolution. I see nothing totalitarian or utopian in the recognition that our values are in urgent need of modification.

In western countries the idea of social justice involving higher taxation for businesses and wealthy citizens and the introduction of social handouts came up against the egoism of those who refused to share their wealth with others. Yet in spite of this a form of capitalism that takes this into account has prevailed in all the developed countries.

In an era of rapid change social awareness also changes very quickly. Even in the last few decades western societies have made noticeable progress in their mentality regarding, to mention only a few changes, the extension of human rights, the overcoming of racism, the emancipation of women, the recognition of childhood, and overall a greater degree of tolerance. In my view, the next change will involve the advent of ecological awareness.

This can be speeded up in various ways: by informing the public about ecological problems including the consequences of military conflict and of poverty; by bringing ecology into schools and universities; and by national and international support for scientific research into protecting the environment.

Many countries have signed up to the Aarhus Convention on access to information on environmental matters. The United Nations programme on protecting the environment and also independent TV channels and film production companies such as TVE which specialize in ecological subjects all support the dissemination of information about aspects of ecology with the help of the internet. Numerous NGOs also use the internet and the print media to disseminate detailed information about protecting the environment.

For most of the mass media, however, such subjects are unimportant or, in some cases, even taboo, especially in countries where the environment is in a bad way. The proceedings against the Russian military journalist Grigori Pasko,[20] who published his researches on the 'disposal' of radioactive waste into the Sea of Japan by the Russian Pacific Fleet, showed once again how difficult it sometimes is to draw the line between a country's legitimate right to keep something secret and the no less legitimate right of humanity everywhere to be given vital information.

The mass media, justifiably called 'the third estate', can function as a bridge between the authorities and the population of any country. Open discussion in the media with representatives of government and public opinion should become the rule in all matters of ecological safety and environmental protection prior to any decision being taken by the state.

The mass media have a decisive role to play in the development of ecological awareness through informing users about accepting restrictions for the sake of protecting the biosphere and, in the last resort, for the sake of preserving life on earth. The European NGO Friends of the Earth has estimated that the EU must reduce its utilization of natural resources by 75 per cent over the coming 30 years if the environment is to be maintained in its present state. It is obvious that such decisive measures can only be taken if the population itself is deeply convinced that they are necessary.

But conviction alone is insufficient. Knowledge is the true key to accepting the principle of sustainability and the development of ecological awareness. Both African farmers and tribes in the Amazon rainforests need help in learning about the best way to till their land. Such methods will then allow them to continue farming without destroying their own environment. But almost all other work now also calls for knowledge about how to protect the environment.

It will be necessary for the citizens of all industrial societies to learn how to save energy and water and how to categorize their waste products. Although this has been going on for some years already the extent of its practice is still far from sufficient. Here is an example: European countries have only now begun to use solar panels for heating water and to apply economical methods of irrigation in fields and gardens such as have already been in use for decades in Israel which, like the whole of the Near East, suffers from an acute shortage of water and lacks its own sources of energy.

In view of the rapid change in circumstances and the possible appearance of new dangers, ecological instruction should begin in school before continuing throughout the whole of life. Children should feel themselves to be citizens not only of their country but of the earth, and learn to think and act accordingly while also gaining knowledge about the environment and practical skills for the life and work necessary in the region where they live.

However, in a world of limited resources, exhausted land and polluted water, air and food, general ecological awareness is only a first step. Over and above this it is our duty to teach some elementary survival techniques to people in poverty-stricken regions who lack access to clean water and scrape an ecologically intolerable living. For despite all our good intentions and programmes to root out poverty, 1.3 billion people living in the slums and industrial districts of developing countries breathe toxic air, and 1.2 billion lack clean drinking water. And 700 million mostly women and children also suffer from air pollution caused by primitive heating systems.

The Belorussian physicist Vasili Nesterenko provides an astonishing example of this. He has founded an independent institute for the protection of the population against radiation. This institute provides information to villagers living near Chernobyl where the soil is still polluted by the radioactive isotope Caesium 137. Members of the institute have trained hundreds of young teachers and nurses who in turn teach the local schoolchildren effective methods of reducing the degree of contamination in locally grown foods.

In order to work out and apply protective measures for the population we need reliable information about current and future risks. When I stated that we are living in an entirely new world and an entirely new phase of human history I was also thinking that despite our impressive information in many fields we still have large gaps in our knowledge about the earth and its main ecosystems.

Scientists simulate the possible consequences of global changes, for example that of climate warming due to gas emissions, and reach the conclusion that the greenhouse effect would lead to the melting of the arctic ice. This might open up a trade route via the North Pole, but at the same time the Gulf Stream would be diverted from its present course or might even disappear, which would make north-western Europe much colder. So economic interests would not be the only consideration, for many millions of lives would also be threatened! International research in this field needs to be co-ordinated as soon as possible to enable us to foresee such consequences in good time.

The package of measures needed to save the earth and improve our lives is surely gigantic. Shall we be able to alter the course of our *Titanic*?

I believe this is not the right way to formulate this question. In all ages there have been men and women who have acted on the basis of their ideals without thinking of any personal advantage. Some of them, such as Charles de Gaulle or Mother Theresa, become world famous. But the majority remain unknown. The force that is driving governments, states and international authorities is the rapidly developing global civil society and the multitude of NGOs, i.e. responsible and motivated citizens of the earth. No one can achieve the impossible alone, but every one of us can contribute our mite to the construction of our commonly owned 'cathedral' by concentrating on the field of activity closest to home.

Princess Basma, sister of the deceased King Hussein of Jordan, is trying to save the unique coral reefs of the Gulf of Aqaba in the Red Sea; the Sierra-Leonian biologist Monty Jones has bred a new, highly resistant and productive species of rice that is already changing the lives of poor farmers in Africa; the American actor Robert Redford has mobilized public opinion against oil extraction in the Arctic; the former Indian Maharaja Fatha Sing Rethor has founded a nature reserve in Rajasthan in order to save the remnants of the jungle and the last Bengal tigers; the French farmer José Bové is fighting against the spread of genetically engineered crops; Nelson Mandela, formerly President of South Africa, has founded the international initiative Cities Without Slums.

I too have chosen a field in which I can work. As though the whole of my life had been a preparation for this, in 1993 I took on the presidency of an international NGO, Green Cross International. This is the 'cross' I have been carrying for the last ten years.

MY GREEN 'CROSS'

Many readers may be asking why it was necessary to found yet another NGO — Green Cross International — dedicated to environmental problems and the struggle for peace and against poverty, when a number of such organizations already exist.

In my view, Green Cross International is original in that we have made connections between the main challenges facing our time, and that we not only undertake practical projects but also maintain a permanent dialogue. This dialogue is carried on between well-known politicians, artists and scientists, representatives of various religions, ecologists and leaders of NGOs on the one hand, and ordinary citizens on the other. We are, after all, living in a new era with its own philosophical stamp and new ethical ideas.

The organization was founded during the Earth Summit attended by heads of government in Rio de Janeiro in 1992. A parallel event was a non-government forum of parliamentarians and cultural activists during which the idea of founding a worldwide NGO called Green Cross International was expressed. I had suggested this title at an international meeting in Moscow in 1987 and it had evidently stuck in someone's mind.

Humanity cannot rely solely on politicians to solve environmental problems and build up a new world order. This era of change calls on people the world over to join forces in their efforts to create a global society capable of forcing governments and economic groupings to include ecological and social factors in their decision-making.

These were the considerations in my mind when I agreed to become the first President of Green Cross International. It came into being a year later, and today it is already active in 26 countries.

Our tasks cover many fields: eco-tourism in the Rio Grande nature reserve in Bolivia; planting willows to detoxify polluted soil in Poland; a campaign for the effective utilization of energy sources in the USA; teaching recycling in the Czech Republic; painting competitions for children on the theme of protecting the environment in Japan; bringing ecology into schools in Russia; and dozens of other projects. But here I want to say a few words about the main thrusts of our work and how they reflect our philosophy, and also about our large international projects.

The ecological consequences of war and other conflicts

In discussing the victims of war, newspapers and history books on the whole concentrate on human and economic victims rather than the ecological consequences. Only recently have people begun to realize that any conflict, even those in which weapons of mass destruction are not deployed, is a war against the environment and life in the wider sense.

Landmines in fields, woods and mountains laid by retreating troops leading to the loss of agricultural land and mineral reserves for the population, quite apart from the loss of human life; the employment of toxic defoliants and poisonous gases against an enemy and thus unavoidably also against the civilian population; pollution of water supplies; the use in modern weaponry of depleted uranium which is normally inactive but turns into a radioactive aerosol when treated grenades hit the metal casing of tanks;[21] blowing up oil storage facilities, oil refineries and chemical plants – all this has been the reality of war in the second half of the twentieth and at the beginning of the twenty-first century in Vietnam and Afghanistan, in Iraq and Kosovo, in Bosnia and Chechnya and dozens of other conflict zones across the world.

The USA used defoliants on 10 per cent of Vietnam's territory. A quarter of a century later 3,500 children are still being born every year with congenital abnormalities: cleft palate, double sets of teeth, serious muscular atrophy – the victims of Agent Orange. And the number of miscarriages, cases of female infertility and urogenital diseases are on the increase.

Gigantic damage was done to the health of Kuwait's population by the burning day and night of 700 boreholes and to the farmers of Iraq by the explosion of 90,000 bombs on their land (1991). We have analysed the consequences of the Gulf War and are convinced that sooner or later the world will have to accept the increase of cancers in Iraq as the result of inhaling radioactive dust.

And how many decades will it take to clear almost a million anti-personnel mines in Bosnia? How many decades until Grozny, the capital city of Chechnya, is rebuilt? Will it ever be possible to remove the oil from the strategic 40 per cent of Kuwait's water resources polluted by Iraqi aggression?

The cold war, too, has left us with grave consequences. There are regions polluted by chemical and radioactive waste that are now more or less uninhabitable both in Russia and in the USA. The pretext of national security kept these facts secret for decades.

Or let us take a look at the map of waste disposal sites to which the waste from still-functioning armaments factories continues to be transported. At the Rocky Flats arsenal not far from the city of Denver in Colorado, for example, 125 types of toxic residue have been stored over a period of 30 years. Nerve gases and pesticides were also produced here. This tract of land has been nicknamed 'the most polluted square mile in the world'. In some parts of Dover in New York State the degree of contamination of the groundwater is 5,000 times greater than the permitted level. According to the former energy minister in America, Billy Richardson, the removal of nuclear and other residues of arms production will cost the USA unknown billions of dollars.

Russia's situation is far more difficult because it simply does not have enough money. The pollution caused by the arms race after the Second World War is one example: From 1952 onwards the liquid residues of the arms industry were stored not far from Lake Karachai in the Urals. Through negligence they seeped into the lake, and now traces can be found thousands of kilometres away in the Arctic. Gradually the thermal energy produced by the residues caused the whole lake to evaporate. The 125 million curies contained in the waste – double the amount of Chernobyl – were then to be found in the air instead. Today the lake is covered by a thick layer of cement, a kind of flat sarcophagus – yet another brush-stroke in the fresco of the apocalypse.

Even the arsenals of nuclear, chemical and biological weapons in the USA, Russia and other states which appear to pose no problems and do no damage to the health of local populations are potentially dangerous.

I cannot forget being instructed in the use of the 'nuclear button' when I was head of state of the Soviet Union. I was shown what had to be done if I was informed of a nuclear attack on one flank and then, while I was considering what to do, if information of another attack on the other flank was received. I was supposed to decide immediately! I have to admit that I never touched that button, even while I was being given these instructions, and even though the little case containing it never left my side.[22]

It is possible to imagine catastrophic scenarios that could come about in connection with chemical or biological weapons. Nerve gas might leak from rusty casings, or such weapons might get into the hands of terrorists. We have already experienced how the regime of Saddam Hussein used toxic gas against Kurds, how the Aum sect attacked the underground in Tokyo with sarin gas in 1995, and how more recently anthrax spores were widely distributed with the help of the American postal system.

The way for humanity to rid itself of such threats is by destroying its nuclear, chemical and biological arsenals as soon as possible. In today's world, where all countries are mutually interdependent, even the most dramatic problems will have to be solved politically and not militarily. I applied these principles of new thinking when I was a head of state and I shall continue to do so now. In the framework of its Legacy Programme, Green Cross International is also taking energetic steps in this direction. Unfortunately the name does not imply a cultural legacy but one of war and the arms race.

Green Cross International supports all initiatives for disarmament and for the elimination of weapons of mass destruction in all countries. In our opinion the United Nations as well as other international associations such as the Organization for Security and Co-operation in Europe should endeavour not only to defuse military conflicts but also to prevent them by keeping an eye on international tensions that could tip over into armed conflict.

If conflict does break out, military operations should at least be prevented from damaging the environment. We therefore suggest that the Geneva Convention could include additional restrictions such as the outlawing of bombardment on certain industrial plants: in the first place nuclear power stations and petro-chemical and chemical plants. Also forbidden should be the use of dangerous weapon types, such as those containing depleted uranium, since their deployment results in long-term damage to human health and the environment. Finally we advocate setting up an international fund that would act in cases where the environment is affected by war or technological catastrophes.

Green Cross International is especially active in connection with the elimination of chemical weapons. Although the convention forbidding the production and storage of chemical weapons has already been signed by 173 countries and was ratified by the American Senate and the Russian Duma several years ago, the USA still possesses about 25,000 tonnes of them, while Russia has 40,000 tonnes located for the most part in the European part of the country.[23] In recent years the USA has destroyed 6,000 tonnes in Utah and on the Johnston Atoll. And other states are also building plants where chemical weapons will be dismantled and eliminated.

The main problem here is the high cost, which is far greater than the cost of production.[24] In the USA this totals about 20 billion dollars, whereas Russia will only need half this amount,[25] but the burden will be heavy nevertheless. In my capacity as President of Green Cross International I have called on the governments of the USA and European countries to aid Russia in this. European and American pledges are encouraging, and President Putin has also managed to obtain an increase in the budget for this purpose. Green Cross International will nevertheless continue to monitor the situation. This 'chemical Carthage' must be annihilated!

Other Green Cross projects within the framework of our Legacy Programme are: participation in the reassignment of military bases and the detoxification of territories polluted by chemical and radioactive substances; dispatch of independent experts to assess the ecological consequences of the Iraq and Kosovo conflicts; providing aid for Vietnamese children with congenital defects caused by the American defoliant Agent Orange; organizing stays in sanatoria for child victims of radioactive and chemical pollution in Russia and Belarus.

Water as a source of conflict, water for peace

A glance at a map of the world might give us the misleading impression that the availability of water cannot possibly be a problem. However, 97 per cent of the earth's water exists in seas and oceans, and desalination of seawater is a costly and not very effective process. For the same reason it would be difficult to make use of the 2 per cent of the world's water locked up in the polar icecaps notwithstanding the tempting suggestion that icebergs could be towed to the coasts of hot countries. Of the remaining 1 per cent, a certain amount is made unusable by floods, evaporation and pollution, which leaves a remainder of about 0.1 per cent of all the earth's water. So 12,500 cubic kilometres of water are available for humanity. At present, 6,400 cubic kilometres are used by 6 billion people, which leaves a reserve of 6,100 cubic kilometres. What will happen to these reserves when there are 9 billion inhabitants of the earth? Moreover, these resources could soon be made scarcer by the effects of global warming, silting up of rivers and lakes, industrial pollution and the extraction of groundwater.

Water has been a source of conflict ever since the time of the ancient Sumerians when the city of Lagash waged war with the state of Umma about the right to build irrigation canals to draw water from the Tigris. The American writer Mark Twain remarked shrewdly that whiskey was an object of drinking while water was an object of conflict. He was referring to semi-desert territories in the Wild West where there had been bloody battles over water. Unfortunately, the mentality of many politicians today has progressed little compared with that of those American cowboys of yore.

In our time, as natural resources are constantly diminishing, many countries are prepared to fight or even wage war for control over them. And since water is the most important source of life, a decrease in its availability could have very tragic consequences. Like religion and ideologies, conflicts about possession of water are likely to unleash the passions of the masses.

Every fifth inhabitant of the earth has no access to clean drinking water today. This situation is especially critical in the Near East, Africa and Central and Southeast Asia. With the dead being cremated along its banks, the Ganges, India's sacred river, is infecting the living with typhus, cholera and ailments of the digestive tract; the great Yellow River in China, which used to flood regularly, is drying up as the result of ever increasing agriculture, industrialization and urbanization.

Humanity will have to reach a consensus about how to settle the matter of national sovereignty in managing the 260 largest and most important rivers and lakes that adjoin the territory of two or more countries. In my opinion national sovereignty should take second place where the utilization of these resources is concerned because the right to have water for drinking is as much an immutable right for every inhabitant of the earth as is the right to have air for breathing. So international collaboration is of paramount importance where water resources are used by more than one country. Of course this will be difficult especially in regions such as the Near East where conflicts and old hatreds have deep roots. Nevertheless, if it was possible for the Berlin Wall to fall, why should the barriers of hatred and mistrust not fall as well?

In the spring of the year 2000 I embarked on a study tour to the Near East where I met with King Abdullah II of Jordan, the then Prime Minister of Israel Ehud Barak, and the President of the Palestinian Authority Yasser Arafat. There were great hopes at the time that a peaceful solution would be found for the region and that a Palestinian state would soon be created. Nevertheless, all three politicians were very worried about the dwindling of potable water resources which seemed to point to future conflicts. I myself was surprised to find the Biblical river Jordan, from which Israelis, Palestinians and Jordanians draw water, to be not much more than a stream. The population of the countries adjoining the Jordan Valley, namely Jordan, Israel, the Palestinian Authority, Lebanon and Syria, now already numbers 35 million. This is likely to double over the next 50 years.

In the past few decades the countries of the Near East have spent billions of dollars on acquiring and producing arms instead of building aqueducts and working out methods for the conservation, purification and effective usage of water in the whole region. Would it not have been cheaper to desalinate or manage water resources communally than wage war about them?

Green Cross uses international negotiation to prevent conflicts about water and is working for access to water to be recognized as a general human right. In line with this logic we are calling for a 'Marshall Plan' for the Near East, for it is often geopolitical interests, especially efforts to gain control of resources, that lie hidden behind the rhetoric of the main participants in the Near East conflict. If we succeed in reducing the inequality in water supplies and thus the dissatisfaction of the population we can push forward towards peace. It is worth noting that the infrastructure needed for supplying water to the population was not damaged even during the last particularly brutal intifada. The political leaders of the region have to understand that, as everywhere else in the world, there can be no one-sided utilization of water supplies that belong to two or more countries. Some kind of co-operation between states is essential.

The Jordan Valley is only one of our numerous projects. The range of Green Cross International's work to prevent conflicts about water and promote effective technologies for purification and usage reaches from the Paraná in South America, via the Okavango and Lake Volta in Africa, to the Danube in Central Europe and the Volga in Russia.

Water can and indeed must become a decisive factor for peace and security. This is one of the most important challenges facing the new century.

A charter for the earth

The United Nations Conference on the Human Environment which took place in Stockholm in 1972 showed that all environmental problems are closely linked with one another.

Changes in the composition of the atmosphere lead to ozone holes, global warming and other forms of climate change. Destruction of the tropical rainforest impairs biodiversity. From Stockholm a call went out to all the nations of the earth to work together in solving environmental problems globally.

My friend Maurice Strong, Chairman of the Earth Council – another non-government organization – described the planet's situation in a remarkable way: 'The earth is an integrative system that transcends the artificial borders of national states. When these states turn their attention to the global problems thrown up by the oceans, the atmosphere and climate change, they can only realize their sovereignty through co-operation with other countries.'

Of course every nation and every state has its own ethical ideas, its own value system and religious convictions, but not even such recognized principles as those of human rights will be adequate as a basis for the achievement of effective co-operation. We need to develop a new value system which takes global environmental problems into account and which provides the whole of humanity – states as well as individuals – with a guideline for action.

Over the last 25 years many personalities in public life, in non-government organizations and international authorities have endeavoured to formulate the principles and values needed for sustainable development with its economic, social and ecological implications. The result of these considerations was the 1992 Rio Declaration on the Environment and

Development. However, despite its fundamental character this declaration did not fulfil the criteria of a genuine charter that could stand like a third pillar together with the Universal Declaration of Human Rights and the United Nations Charter.

Shortly after the Rio Earth Summit, Maurice Strong and I launched an important initiative. The Earth Council and Green Cross International began a series of comprehensive international consultations in order to work out a charter for the earth. After three years of hard work the international committee consisting of widely respected individuals had laid down the fundamental principles of this document. And then over 100,000 individuals in more than 50 countries participated in producing the final version.

The Jewish sage Hillel formulated the essence of Judaism in a single sentence: 'Do not to your neighbour that which you abominate.' Jesus Christ clothed humanity's most important moral principle in similar words. On this idea are founded the Ten Commandments that form the fundamental law of the three great monotheistic religions.

The basic idea of the Earth Charter can also be summarized in a single sentence: 'To save humanity and all future generations we must save the earth.' The 16 Principles of the Charter encompass the environment, human rights, overcoming poverty, equality of the sexes, and education for a culture of peace.

This document, which on the one hand provides humanity

with a legislative framework for sustainable development and on the other can serve as an excellent textbook for a new ethic, was published in Paris on 12 March 2000. Although we hope that sooner or later the Charter will be adopted by the United Nations as an instruction book for action, we are under no illusion as to the workings of international bureaucracy. Not one ecological initiative has so far been launched from the labyrinth of the United Nations, the corridors of governmental power or the anterooms of ministers even though the present state of our biosphere is calling for immediate action.

So this document is directed in the first instance to the global community of citizens. I am quite convinced that if the global community does not take its fate into its own hands, all the suggestions will rest for years on the shelves of the United Nations and other international organizations, gathering dust and being suffocated by endless discussions and financial delaying tactics.

Many people feel discouraged nowadays. They are worried about their security and made anxious by unemployment, poverty, epidemics, international terrorism, violence, natural or man-made catastrophes, the too-rapid speed of change, and the potential of dangerous developments in science such as genetic engineering and cloning. They look with pessimism towards their future and that of their children. In such situations some people withdraw into their shell in order to fend off the global problems which anyway make them feel utterly helpless. But this is a dangerous thing to do. With the help of the Earth Charter we want to rouse people and mobilize them to fight for their own future. Our Charter gives people the ethical and moral points of orientation so urgently needed at the threshold of the new millennium.

What has happened to ethical ideas?

Work on the Earth Charter caused me to think about questions of ethics and their relation to environmental problems. After all, discussions about ecology have been going on for 30 years; important decisions and agreements have been made on international, national, regional and local levels, and these have been honoured by numerous enterprises. Nevertheless not a single arrangement has been fully realized. There have been some partial successes, such as protection of the ozone hole, but in fact it has not been possible to stop the deterioration.

Why is it that so many of these accepted, sensible and essential decisions are not being followed? Is it perhaps because, unlike the practical aspects, the moral and ethical considerations concerning sustainable development are not properly recognized? Could attention to the ethical principles help us save the world?

Maurice Strong and I invited participation in an international forum, the Earth Dialogue in Lyon in January 2002 which was concerned with all these questions. In view of the growing anti-globalization movement and the recognition now enjoyed everywhere by civil society, this dialogue between all representatives of public life was urgently necessary. That is why – in contrast to Davos and Porto Allegre – Green Cross International and the Earth Council invited 180 representatives of international organizations from politics, economics and industry, journalists, parliamentarians, officers from various churches, representatives of non-government organizations and former ministers for foreign affairs *all together*, to have dialogues among themselves and with over 1,500 participants in the forum.

We hoped that a few months before the Johannesburg World Summit on Sustainable Development the forum participants would make efforts towards identifying the main obstacles to realizing Agenda 21 and discuss new challenges and possibilities that had appeared since the Earth Summit of 1992.

So many – practical and utopian – ideas were put forward in Lyon! Give every citizen of the earth access to the internet in order to build a virtual bridge between rich and poor countries, between doctors and patients, between farmers and agrarian scientists, and between teachers and the children of the savannahs or the rainforests of the Amazon Basin; found an international information authority for environmental matters in every country to disseminate ecological knowledge specifically among children; achieve equal representation of all countries in the international organizations; reform the World Trade Organization because at present it is trying to impose a symmetrical pattern on an asymmetrical world, whereas it ought to be making decisions that discriminate positively in favour of economically weaker countries; teach respect for the earth and the universe in schools; completely revise the relationship between humans and the earth; intensify inter-faith dialogue; make the distribution of subsidies to industry dependent on social and economic criteria. Hundreds of other suggestions were also written down during the three days of the Forum.

Of course no one expected solutions to the complex problems confronting humanity to be conjured up from one minute to the next. But we did indeed achieve what was most important which was that for the first time ever representatives of all sections of worldwide public opinion met for a discussion. It was decided to set up a permanent forum on sustainable development on the internet, to be activated after the Johannesburg summit. This will enable considerations about our common future to continue or, in other words, we have succeeded in setting the planetary 'ant hill' in motion.

After I had proclaimed glasnost and perestroika in the USSR, Soviet society began to effervesce and bubble, and within five years a radical change had taken place across the world. The map of the world changed, as did people's values and the politics of the world.

Now millions of people are demanding a policy of transparency and of transformation in our mutual life on the earth. We want every inhabitant of the 'global village' to have access to information about what is going on and thus be enabled to participate in the gigantic perestroika of the twenty-first century — the revolution in values and awareness — for otherwise every measure will be condemned to failure.

In 1917 the great poet Velimir Khlebnikov declared himself and every other creative person to be 'presidents of the terrestrial globe'. At the same time he also spoke out against war and against the power held by states and governments over the individual who was anyway only being led to the slaughterhouse by them. Today it is my dream that every aware citizen should be 'a president of the earth' and take responsibility for its fate upon himself or herself.

HOMO SAPIENS OR ROBOT SAPIENS?

The Book of Genesis tells how God placed Adam and Eve into the Garden of Eden. He permitted them to eat the fruit of all the trees except the Tree of Knowledge. But Adam and Eve disobeyed him and ate of the forbidden fruit. Thereupon God drove them out of Paradise and made Adam earn his living by the sweat of his brow.

I have often wondered about the meaning of this story from the Bible. It seems to mirror in symbolic form the transition from the stage when man with all the other creatures of the earth utilized the riches of nature passively to the stage when nature had to be actively worked upon with the help of tools. But only in the past few hundred years has humanity become a force that can considerably alter the face of the earth — a force, as Vladimir Vernadsky put it, of geology.

Human beings have now taken over the whole planet. They have covered its surface with large and small towns, moving more soil in the process than was ever moved by all former tectonic shifts. They have dug up forests, changed the course of rivers, destroyed animal and plant species and bred new ones, and changed the climate.

In Vernadsky's opinion such gigantic changes cannot have come about by accident: 'The biosphere is changing radically before our very eyes. And there can be no doubt that being dependent on the will of human beings, the transformation which is expressing itself in this way is no accidental phenomenon but a *spontaneous process of nature*, the roots of which lie deeply buried, having been prepared by an evolutionary process lasting hundreds of millions of years. This transformation is coming about as a result of scientific thinking and by means of organized human endeavour.'[26]

If we accept the view of this great scientist who was a proponent of scientific determinism, if we believe that our actions, which have transformed the earth, are merely consequences of the laws of evolution, then perhaps there is no point in becoming alarmed about the state of our earthly home.

Early in the twentieth century the famous Russian painter and innovator Kazimir Malevich was dreaming of transforming not only nature but also the human being and, in the final analysis, of overcoming death: 'How magnificent are the brightly-coloured birds in the virgin forests of Ceylon. But no less beautiful are the aeroplanes in the virgin realms of space of today . . . We shall have to adapt to the reorganization. Perhaps there will no longer be any air, so that our lungs, like motorcars, will breathe petrol . . . Human beings must still work hard at their organism in order to reach the perfection attained by machines in the form of the locomotive. For this can be taken apart and all its inner workings removed and replaced by new ones, and then it will come to life again.'[27]

Such dreams have become reality in our time. We have learned to transplant organs and are in the process of mastering the cloning of organs and indeed of the whole human being. Computer chips are implanted in the human body that enable us to test our state of health, and in the future they will allow us to achieve a synthesis between the computer's brain and the human brain. Many American experts on artificial intelligence and robotic technology are convinced that robots will be a future stage of evolution and that *robot sapiens* will be the next stage after *homo sapiens*, even by the end of the present century. The researcher Hans Moravek of the American Carnegie-Mellon University describes a future in which the human race will be knocked off its throne by its own artificial descendants.

Mechanical or bionic robots will not need clean air; they will manage without water or food and learn to draw their energy directly from the sun. They will be able to manage without the beauty of a sunset over the steppe or salt-laden gusts of wind on the seashore as well as without the music of Mozart or the paintings of Michelangelo. *Our* civilization, however, and *our* heritage from our ancestors, and we ourselves are not perfect even though we call ourselves the crown of creation; and for us there will be no place in that new and from *our* point of view horrible world.

Is this path of evolution really to be our destiny? A good many scientists doubt the deterministic principle of evolution and the all-too 'linear' Darwinistic theory of the evolution of species. For example the important American palaeontologist Stephen Jay Gould, recently deceased, made a thorough analysis of the evolution of life on the earth and of the main branches in the history of how the species evolved. He believed that the dinosaurs were extremely well adapted to their environment and that the mammals would have had no chance of becoming the dominant race if an asteroid or comet had not collided with the earth causing a radical climate change that resulted in the dinosaurs becoming extinct. According to Gould the arrival of the human being is an almost unbelievable coincidence, a detail in history and in no way a manifestation of some general law.[28]

If the human being arrived on the earth entirely by accident, if it would indeed have been possible for the continents to shelter only plants and insects and for the dinosaurs to rule the world, surely this renders our human civilization especially precious and unique. But if we consider the speed with which we are destroying our environment and bringing forth golems and Frankenstein monsters who might escape our control at any moment, then the inevitable questions arise: In contrast to the theories of Vernadsky and other proponents of determinism, is our feverish effort in the name of 'progress' going to end in a cul-de-sac of history? Are we standing on the threshold of a new expulsion from Paradise which would make not only the individual but the whole of humanity mortal?

There is no answer to this question, but in the end every

living creature does possess an instinct for self-preservation, and we humans are no exception. That is why we must leave the earth undamaged, why we must try to cope with the evil genies we have let out of the bottle and hope that they will come to heel.

The many essential measures to be taken are so comprehensive and the biosphere is such a complex system that some scientists are already beginning to doubt whether it will be possible to regulate the life processes of the earth. For example the Russian biologist K. Lossev writes: 'The biosphere has existed for four billion years. Throughout this enormous period of time it regulated all its systems with the greatest accuracy and created optimal conditions for all the life forms that existed at every stage of evolution. This took care of the dynamic durability of the environment and the genomes of the organism. Then the human being appeared and made use of the fossil fuels (i.e. the surplus energy which the biosphere had formerly withdrawn from the environment in order to retain its sustainability) and began with their help to destroy the biosphere without considering the consequences. Meanwhile, initial investigations into the biosphere as an integral system have shown that it is infinitely more complex than human civilization. In it there flow information currents which regulate the environment. Their capacity is many times greater than future possibilities of dealing with the information currents of civilization. So it is hardly likely that humanity will ever be able to comprehend the complexity of this system, let alone regulate it.'[29]

This touches on one of life's greatest mysteries. Perhaps the religious philosophy of Buddhism comes closest to understanding it since it includes the human being in the general cycle of nature and all living things as well as regarding all life forms as sacred. But respect for life is not the preserve of Buddhism alone. Nowadays humanity, so multifarious within its oneness, needs a new philosophy of life, a new ethic that can shape the fundamental values which are common to all religions and which rest upon the consensus of all the peoples of the earth. Some very different well-known personalities have already called for such a 'global ethic' to be elaborated: Pope John Paul II, the Jordanian Prince Hassan bin Tallal, and the Burmese Nobel Peace laureate Aung San Suu Kyi. I would like to add my voice to theirs.

There is no point in assuming that we can regulate life. But on the basis of our good sense and our feelings, our knowledge, our love of life and of our neighbour, our faith and our ability to work we can endeavour to retain most of what still remains and learn to respect life rather than destroying it, and thus ensure the survival of humanity.

Like the great American writer William Faulkner I refuse to accept the possibility of an end to humanity – whatever trials it might still face.

This is my credo – the credo of an incorrigible optimist.

Afterword

After the World Summit on Sustainable Development

Since the first edition of this book was published so many important events and developments have occurred all over the world that I should like to take this opportunity to add a postscript.

Over the past few months the brutal attacks on Bali, in Mombasa and in my hometown of Moscow have brought a shocking escalation in terrorist activity. Such excesses have not occurred since 11 September 2001, which fundamentally changed the worldwide geopolitical situation. They affect every continent, turn airports and towns into fortresses and stir up fear and uncertainty.

These tensions have been intensified by the war in Iraq which has shocked the international community and is threatening to weaken the cohesion of the United Nations, the very cohesion that we urgently need in order to avert future threats of violence and terror.

In addition, the event has meanwhile taken place that was still the object of copious speculation and scepticism while I was writing the book: the World Summit on Sustainable

Development in Johannesburg in August/September 2002. Reactions to it have been mixed, for it was only partially successful. Nevertheless, the principle of sustainability did attain a higher profile, various very important agreements were reached on fundamental problems such as the availability of potable water, and a number of regional initiatives and strategies were launched. But the Summit failed in that it did not honestly and courageously face up to the critical matters of poverty and ecology – first and foremost climate change – but preferred to give priority to the self-interest of states and disappointing compromises. In short, the Johannesburg Summit achieved more than many had expected but far less than others had hoped.

Many battles still remain to be fought, each of which will call for greater international solidarity and commitment, for with every new attack our common battle against terrorism will intensify. We must protect the role of the United Nations as the only body permitted to decide when and whether diplomatic efforts have been exhausted. In addition, the struggle against poverty, sickness and pollution must be emphatically pursued in order to secure the survival of humanity on the earth.

This battle is perhaps the most important of all, and its outcome will directly affect all the other battles still to be fought. The many millions of people who live miserable lives all over the world in slums, refugee camps and inaccessible rural locations deserve a chance to develop and become actively involved in the globalized world. What can encourage them to support democracy, tolerance and peace in place of violence and extremism if wealthy countries maintain trade restrictions and agricultural subsidies while ignoring the consequences of their own wasteful ways and their dependence on fossil fuels? Faced with selfish attitudes in connection with debt release and the availability of essential medicines, why should such people not become indignant? They merely see that human life is not everywhere measured by the same yardstick. Poverty is of itself a terrible form of violence against humanity. Those having to manage without clean water and basic medical care are not living in peace. Like war, poverty destroys life and fans the flames of dissatisfaction.

With so much at stake, we had hoped that the Johannesburg Summit would yield more suggestions on countering the causes of terrorism in many developing countries. But in the end the delegates and political leaders from the 181 countries represented lacked the decisiveness and vision to confront the true challenges of averting ecological disasters, fighting the scourge of poverty and creating a really worthwhile future for all by means of sustainable development.

This is not solely a matter of dismantling weapons arsenals, seeking out terrorists or removing the political leaders who support them. The question is how to deal with the causes of conflict, i.e. with the inequality existing in the world, with the unfair distribution and redistribution of wealth, with the failure to recognize international rights and fundamental human rights, or to satisfy the basic needs of more than two billion people for example for water, energy and education. The poor require an opportunity to win back their dignity. Otherwise the inequality between poor and rich, between North and South and insufficient adherence to democratic principles will prepare the soil for all forms of terrorism and extremism.

I find it profoundly disappointing that the hopes for a new world order which so many entertained after the collapse of the Soviet Union at the end of the 1980s and the beginning of the 1990s have come to nothing. The world has missed a unique opportunity to change the fate of the earth. It is now up to us to work harder than ever to bring about another such opportunity, and we need to employ all the means we have at our disposal.

The Summit on Sustainable Development was one such opportunity, but the world community failed to make sufficient use of it. The press and all the other media were sceptical from the start and their interest was limited.

Many representatives of the media and opinion leaders have tried to over-simplify the matter and blame the United States for the failure of the Summit. But this estimation is incorrect. In the matter of climate change, for example, the USA found allies against the EU and non-government organizations among the producers of fossil fuels; yet in another matter, that of agricultural subsidies and debt release, the

USA and the EU formed an alliance. The world is not Manichaean, and no country should shoulder all the blame.

Ten years after the 1992 Earth Summit in Rio de Janeiro, this new meeting provided an opportunity to re-evaluate the world situation as to environmental, developmental, social and economic questions. Most of the delegates admitted that not enough had been done in the interim and that the world was marching on the spot instead of forwards. So what was, in fact, achieved in Johannesburg?

The Millennium Development Goals set by the United Nations were confirmed in the Summit's political declaration. Water heads the world's priority list so that the provision of potable water and of basic sanitation for everyone is now recognized as an essential measure for combating poverty. This is the only clear success of the Johannesburg action plan. Once the US had given up its obstinate resistance, the heads of government agreed to aim at halving the number of people lacking basic sanitation (2.4 billion) by 2015. If this succeeds it could mean considerable improvement for the poor, since two million people, mainly children, die every year from polluted drinking water. So we must now ensure that this commitment is kept.

Although water was one of the subjects most successfully dealt with by the Summit, an important aspect was deliberately by-passed, namely that of the international watercourses. Nothing at all was said about the joint management and creation of conflict-solving mechanisms for the 260 international rivers and their catchment areas inhabited by 40 per cent of the world's population. This is another step backwards from Rio where international water management was expressly discussed. Although access to water was confirmed as a worldwide priority, some of the developing countries lacked the political will to commit to joint management of this important resource.

The Earth Charter was mentioned in the draft of the Summit's political declaration: 'We take note of the challenges discussed in the Earth Charter.' However, that draft was revised twice and those words no longer appeared in the final text. Nevertheless the very fact that reference was made to the Earth Charter at all was a victory, for it meant that people recognized that international decisions about sustainability needed an ethical framework. Representatives of ten to 15 countries and several heads of state mentioned the Earth Charter. Some, for example French President Chirac and Mexican President Fox, gave convincing and visionary speeches.

The greatest disappointment of the Summit was, however, the outcome of the talks on the energy question. The USA and the OPEC countries were not prepared to set goals for renewable energies. They rejected a suggestion put forward by Brazil and supported, among others, by the remaining Latin American states: to raise the use of clean energy to 10 per cent by 2010.

The Summit decided that the most important fund for

environmental problems, the Global Environment Facility, should support the struggle against desertification which was now threatening a third of the planet's land mass. The countries represented at the Summit also committed themselves to replenish fish stocks 'where possible' by 2025, but critics were of the opinion that existing agreements would be undermined by this. The delegates refused to let agricultural subsidies expire or to demand a fair trade in organic produce, and they took no measures to prevent genetically modified produce from being marketed.

A 'clear reduction' in the extinction of species is planned by 2010. However, this formulation is much weaker than the commitment 'to halt and reverse the present alarming loss of biodiversity' that the governments of the world agreed on when they ratified the Convention on Biodiversity ten years ago.

The Summit also promised 'to promote and support', rather than actually set up, a ten-year programme to curb excessive consumption in the rich countries. The EU pushed for such a programme but the USA, Canada, Australia and Japan opposed it emphatically.

Surprising progress was made in the matter of corporate responsibility chiefly because pressure groups had ensured inclusion of the subject on the agenda. In the end the governments accepted that binding rules governing the behaviour of multinational corporations should be elaborated. The United States opposed this energetically and even took refuge in various obstructive manoeuvres to get itself exempted from the agreement once the initiative had been decided. But the action plan anyway failed to reach the point when deadlines for its implementation would have been set or even required them to be set.

So-called Type II initiatives – partnerships between NGOs, the private sector, governments and international institutions to implement practical measures to combat crises – were not as successful as had been expected. There are at present only about 220 partnerships, on which 235 million dollars are to be spent. What they will actually achieve remains to be seen, but they represent a new factor for the United Nations because they include the rest of society. Green Cross International is participating in three partnerships – this being in keeping with its intention to ease and promote every kind of collaboration.

On 3 September 2002 Rigoberta Menchu Tum and Green Cross International published the Johannesburg Joint Declaration of Nobel Peace Laureates in the presence of Jean-Michel Cousteau and representatives of the mayors of Lyon, Ouagadougou and Curitiba. This called on heads of state and governments to fulfil their political responsibilities and make sustainable development a reality. The mayors of Cape Town and London have since also endorsed the Joint Declaration.

Global politics are in crisis, and United Nations summits of this kind have reached the limit of their effectiveness. Since Johannesburg many have asked whether such summits are a waste of time and doomed to fail. Whatever the answer to this may be, this particular Summit has once more put sustainable development and the environment back on the public and political agenda. This in itself is most important. Nevertheless, it is obvious that the way these conferences are run needs some thorough re-thinking.

Green Cross International is fighting energetically to prevent or end conflicts that arise as a result of environmental damage. It is also helping those who are suffering from the ecological consequences of wars and armed conflicts. Recognition of our work and the use of our analyses and suggestions at the Johannesburg Summit encourage us to persevere in our determination to strive for a sustainable world for all.

Future generations will judge us according to what we achieve today. If we leave nothing but empty promises and missed opportunities behind us we shall deserve to be mercilessly condemned. Meanwhile the number is growing of people and governments all over the world who see the need for change. It is not too late to engender the necessary political will and solidarity to overcome the instability and inequality in the world and build a peaceful future.

Mikhail Gorbachev
Moscow, December 2002

THE EARTH CHARTER[30]

Preamble

We stand at a critical moment in Earth's history, a time when humanity must choose its future. As the world becomes increasingly interdependent and fragile, the future at once holds great peril and great promise. To move forward we must recognize that in the midst of a magnificent diversity of cultures and life forms we are one human family and one Earth community with a common destiny. We must join together to bring forth a sustainable global society founded on respect for nature, universal human rights, economic justice, and a culture of peace. Towards this end, it is imperative that we, the peoples of Earth, declare our responsibility to one another, to the greater community of life, and to future generations.

Earth, Our Home

Humanity is part of a vast evolving universe. Earth, our home, is alive with a unique community of life. The forces of nature make existence a demanding and uncertain adventure, but Earth has provided the conditions essential to life's evolution.

The resilience of the community of life and the well-being of humanity depend upon preserving a healthy biosphere with all its ecological systems, a rich variety of plants and animals, fertile soils, pure waters, and clean air. The global environment with its finite resources is a common concern of all peoples. The protection of Earth's vitality, diversity, and beauty is a sacred trust.

The Global Situation

The dominant patterns of production and consumption are causing environmental devastation, the depletion of resources, and a massive extinction of species. Communities are being undermined. The benefits of development are not shared equitably and the gap between rich and poor is widening. Injustice, poverty, ignorance, and violent conflict are widespread and the cause of great suffering. An unprecedented rise in human population has overburdened ecological and social systems. The foundations of global security are threatened. These trends are perilous—but not inevitable.

The Challenges Ahead

The choice is ours: form a global partnership to care for Earth and one another or risk the destruction of ourselves and the diversity of life. Fundamental changes are needed in our values, institutions, and ways of living. We must realize that when basic needs have been met, human development is primarily about being more, not having more. We have the knowledge and technology to provide for all and to reduce our impacts on the environment. The emergence of a global civil society is creating new opportunities to build a democratic and humane world. Our environmental, economic, political, social, and spiritual challenges are interconnected, and together we can forge inclusive solutions.

Universal Responsibility

To realize these aspirations, we must decide to live with a sense of universal responsibility, identifying ourselves with the whole Earth community as well as our local communities. We are at once citizens of different nations and of one world in which the local and global are linked. Everyone shares responsibility for the present and future well being of the human family and the larger living world. The spirit of human solidarity and kinship with all life is strengthened when we live with reverence for the mystery of being, gratitude for the gift of life, and humility regarding the human place in nature.

We urgently need a shared vision of basic values to provide an ethical foundation for the emerging world community. Therefore, together in hope we affirm the following interdependent principles for a sustainable way of life as a common standard by which the conduct of all individuals, organizations, businesses, governments, and transnational institutions is to be guided and assessed.

Principles

I. Respect and care for the community of life

1. Respect Earth and life in all its diversity.
   a. Recognize that all beings are interdependent and every form of life has value regardless of its worth to human beings.
   b. Affirm faith in the inherent dignity of all human beings and in the intellectual, artistic, ethical, and spiritual potential of humanity.

2. Care for the community of life with understanding, compassion, and love.
   a. Accept that with the right to own, manage, and use natural resources comes the duty to prevent environmental harm and to protect the rights of people.
   b. Affirm that with increased freedom, knowledge, and power comes increased responsibility to promote the common good.

3. Build democratic societies that are just, participatory, sustainable, and peaceful.
   a. Ensure that communities at all levels guarantee

human rights and fundamental freedoms and provide everyone an opportunity to realize his or her full potential.

b. Promote social and economic justice, enabling all to achieve a secure and meaningful livelihood that is ecologically responsible.

4. Secure Earth's bounty and beauty for present and future generations.

a. Recognize that the freedom of action of each generation is qualified by the needs of future generations.

b. Transmit to future generations values, traditions, and institutions that support the long-term flourishing of Earth's human and ecological communities.

In order to fulfill these four broad commitments, it is necessary to:

II. Ecological integrity

5. Protect and restore the integrity of Earth's ecological systems, with special concern for biological diversity and the natural processes that sustain life.

a. Adopt at all levels sustainable development plans and regulations that make environmental conservation and rehabilitation integral to all development initiatives.

b. Establish and safeguard viable nature and biosphere reserves, including wild lands and marine areas, to protect Earth's life support systems, maintain bio-diversity, and preserve our natural heritage.

c. Promote the recovery of endangered species and eco-systems.

d. Control and eradicate non-native or genetically mod-ified organisms harmful to native species and the environment, and prevent introduction of such harmful organisms.

e. Manage the use of renewable resources such as water, soil, forest products, and marine life in ways that do not exceed rates of regeneration and that protect the health of ecosystems.

f. Manage the extraction and use of non-renewable resources such as minerals and fossil fuels in ways that minimize depletion and cause no serious environmental damage.

6. Prevent harm as the best method of environmental pro-tection and, when knowledge is limited, apply a pre-cautionary approach.

a. Take action to avoid the possibility of serious or irre-versible environmental harm even when scientific knowledge is incomplete or inconclusive.

b. Place the burden of proof on those who argue that a proposed activity will not cause significant harm, and make the responsible parties liable for environmental harm.

c. Ensure that decision making addresses the cumulative, long-term, indirect, long distance, and global consequences of human activities.

d. Prevent pollution of any part of the environment and allow no build-up of radioactive, toxic, or other hazardous substances.

e. Avoid military activities damaging to the environment.

7. Adopt patterns of production, consumption, and reproduction that safeguard Earth's regenerative capacities, human rights, and community well being.

a. Reduce, reuse, and recycle the materials used in production and consumption systems, and ensure that residual waste can be assimilated by ecological systems.

b. Act with restraint and efficiency when using energy, and rely increasingly on renewable energy sources such as solar and wind.

c. Promote the development, adoption, and equitable transfer of environmentally sound technologies.

d. Internalize the full environmental and social costs of goods and services in the selling price, and enable consumers to identify products that meet the highest social and environmental standards.

e. Ensure universal access to health care that fosters reproductive health and responsible reproduction.

    f. Adopt lifestyles that emphasize the quality of life and material sufficiency in a finite world.

8. Advance the study of ecological sustainability and promote the open exchange and wide application of the knowledge acquired.

    a. Support international scientific and technical cooperation on sustainability, with special attention to the needs of developing nations.

    b. Recognize and preserve the traditional knowledge and spiritual wisdom in all cultures that contribute to environmental protection and human well being.

    c. Ensure that information of vital importance to human health and environmental protection, including genetic information, remains available in the public domain.

III. *Social and economic justice*

9. Eradicate poverty as an ethical, social, and environmental imperative.

    a. Guarantee the right to potable water, clean air, food security, uncontaminated soil, shelter, and safe sanitation, allocating the national and international resources required.

    b. Empower every human being with the education and resources to secure a sustainable livelihood, and provide social security and safety nets for those who are unable to support themselves.

c. Recognize the ignored, protect the vulnerable, serve those who suffer, and enable them to develop their capacities and to pursue their aspirations.

10. Ensure that economic activities and institutions at all levels promote human development in an equitable and sustainable manner.
   a. Promote the equitable distribution of wealth within nations and among nations.
   b. Enhance the intellectual, financial, technical, and social resources of developing nations, and relieve them of onerous international debt.
   c. Ensure that all trade supports sustainable resource use, environmental protection, and progressive labor standards.
   d. Require multinational corporations and international financial organizations to act transparently in the public good, and hold them accountable for the consequences of their activities.

11. Affirm gender equality and equity as prerequisites to sustainable development and ensure universal access to education, health care, and economic opportunity.
   a. Secure the human rights of women and girls and end all violence against them.
   b. Promote the active participation of women in all aspects of economic, political, civil, social, and cul-

tural life as full and equal partners, decision makers, leaders, and beneficiaries.

c. Strengthen families and ensure the safety and loving nurture of all family members.

12. Uphold the right of all, without discrimination, to a natural and social environment supportive of human dignity, bodily health, and spiritual well being, with special attention to the rights of indigenous peoples and minorities.

a. Eliminate discrimination in all its forms, such as that based on race, color, sex, sexual orientation, religion, language, and national, ethnic or social origin.

b. Affirm the right of indigenous peoples to their spirituality, knowledge, lands and resources and to their related practice of sustainable livelihoods.

c. Honor and support the young people of our communities, enabling them to fulfill their essential role in creating sustainable societies.

d. Protect and restore outstanding places of cultural and spiritual significance.

IV. *Democracy, nonviolence, and peace*

13. Strengthen democratic institutions at all levels, and provide transparency and accountability in governance, inclusive participation in decision making, and access to justice.

a. Uphold the right of everyone to receive clear and timely information on environmental matters and all development plans and activities which are likely to affect them or in which they have an interest.

b. Support local, regional and global civil society, and promote the meaningful participation of all interested individuals and organizations in decision making.

c. Protect the rights to freedom of opinion, expression, peaceful assembly, association, and dissent.

d. Institute effective and efficient access to administrative and independent judicial procedures, including remedies and redress for environmental harm and the threat of such harm.

e. Eliminate corruption in all public and private institutions.

f. Strengthen local communities, enabling them to care for their environments, and assign environmental responsibilities to the levels of government where they can be carried out most effectively.

14. Integrate into formal education and life-long learning the knowledge, values, and skills needed for a sustainable way of life.

a. Provide all, especially children and youth, with educational opportunities that empower them to contribute actively to sustainable development.

b. Promote the contribution of the arts and humanities as well as the sciences in sustainability education.

c. Enhance the role of the mass media in raising awareness of ecological and social challenges.

d. Recognize the importance of moral and spiritual education for sustainable living.

15. Treat all living beings with respect and consideration.

a. Prevent cruelty to animals kept in human societies and protect them from suffering.

b. Protect wild animals from methods of hunting, trapping, and fishing that cause extreme, prolonged, or avoidable suffering.

c. Avoid or eliminate to the full extent possible the taking or destruction of non-targeted species.

16. Promote a culture of tolerance, nonviolence, and peace.

a. Encourage and support mutual understanding, solidarity, and cooperation among all peoples and within and among nations.

b. Implement comprehensive strategies to prevent violent conflict and use collaborative problem solving to manage and resolve environmental conflicts and other disputes.

c. Demilitarize national security systems to the level of a non-provocative defense posture, and convert military resources to peaceful purposes, including ecological restoration.

d. Eliminate nuclear, biological, and toxic weapons and other weapons of mass destruction.

e. Ensure that the use of orbital and outer space supports environmental protection and peace.

f. Recognize that peace is the wholeness created by right relationships with oneself, other persons, other cultures, other life, Earth, and the larger whole of which all are a part.

The way forward

As never before in history, common destiny beckons us to seek a new beginning. Such renewal is the promise of these Earth Charter principles. To fulfill this promise, we must commit ourselves to adopt and promote the values and objectives of the Charter.

This requires a change of mind and heart. It requires a new sense of global interdependence and universal responsibility. We must imaginatively develop and apply the vision of a sustainable way of life locally, nationally, regionally, and globally. Our cultural diversity is a precious heritage and different cultures will find their own distinctive ways to realize the vision. We must deepen and expand the global dialogue that generated the Earth Charter, for we have much to learn from the ongoing collaborative search for truth and wisdom.

Life often involves tensions between important values. This

can mean difficult choices. However, we must find ways to harmonize diversity with unity, the exercise of freedom with the common good, short-term objectives with long-term goals. Every individual, family, organization, and community has a vital role to play. The arts, sciences, religions, educational institutions, media, businesses, non-governmental organizations, and governments are all called to offer creative leadership. The partnership of government, civil society, and business is essential for effective governance.

In order to build a sustainable global community, the nations of the world must renew their commitment to the United Nations, fulfill their obligations under existing international agreements, and support the implementation of Earth Charter principles with an international legally binding instrument on environment and development.

Let ours be a time remembered for the awakening of a new reverence for life, the firm resolve to achieve sustainability, the quickening of the struggle for justice and peace, and the joyful celebration of life.

INTERVIEW

In November 2002 *Paris Match* invited Mikhail Gorbachev and the French environmental activist and author Nicolas Hulot to join in sounding the alarm for the environment.

Nicolas Hulot: Mr Gorbachev, I'm delighted to meet you, for you impress me greatly as being one of only a few statesmen to have had such a positive influence on the course of contemporary history. I said the same to Nelson Mandela when I met him a few months ago.

PARIS MATCH: Thank you, Nicolas Hulot and Mikhail Gorbachev for being with us here today. It will be wonderful to listen to your conversation for it's rare to hear two such great men talking together. Our subject today is the future of the earth. Each of you has published a manifesto: Mr Gorbachev, your *Manifesto for the Earth*, and Monsieur Hulot, your *Combien de catastrophes avant d'agir? Manifeste pour l'environnement*. Two books, two manifestos, two men from different generations and different cultures but with a mutual desire to save the earth.

Mikhail Gorbachev: Are we really so very different?

PARIS MATCH: We shall see!

M.G.: Russian and European culture — especially that of France and Germany — are very close, for they belong to the same civilization. Almost all world religions were represented in the USSR and 220 languages were spoken there. It is the same in Europe where one hears many different languages spoken by its citizens as well as by immigrants. So the main difference between myself and Monsieur Hulot is our age. But I rather assume that we are looking at the same world with the same problems, so our conclusions and views may not be so very different.

N.H.: We have followed two different paths that had nothing in common. And yet surprisingly we have reached the same conclusions, the same questions and the same hopes.

PARIS MATCH: Before we begin I should like to tell you, Mr Gorbachev, that although we in France know you as the father of Perestroika and as a man of historical stature we are not necessarily aware that you are an environmentalist. May I ask how it is possible to become green after having been red?

M.G.: Well, pale red! And I'm still pale red, by which I mean a social-democrat. But I have to confess to having been bright red once upon a time. For my school-leaving exam I wrote an essay entitled 'Stalin, our glory'. I have a long life behind me, and I've seen much and had to prove much in order to get things changed. Life hasn't been easy, but an easy life lacks concepts and ideas. So our wish for the young must be that they will have a full and fulfilled life. I should like to turn once more to what Monsieur Hulot just said. We happen to be sitting here with you, but there are many people who have written about our subject and who are worried about the future of the earth. Cousteau, for example, has made us think about nature and about what can and does happen to it. And Green Cross International has made it its business to help the many people on the earth who lack potable water. The twentieth century brought many catastrophes with which it has burdened the planet. It was a very brutal century in which also the world wars had consequences for ecology; and then there are the gas emissions and the pollution of the oceans and so on. Even today many rivers are polluted – but what a horrendous muddle! That is why it's no longer enough just to write books.

PARIS MATCH: Was it Chernobyl that converted you to environmental conservation, or was it the ecological disaster of the Soviet Union, and among other things the arms race?

M.G.: No, when I was young the economy had been destroyed by the war, and I became a combine-harvester driver. For two years there was drought in the Stavropol region, and sand-storms which are worse than snowstorms because they leave the fields in a terrible state. In 1948 when this happened I was 17 years old, and that was the first event that made a real impression on me. Later I became a delegate to the Supreme Soviet and a member of the Committee for Environmental

Conservation. That was when I grasped what was going on. Do you know how that committee worked? During a session we each had a file in front of us containing data on the ecological problem under discussion. As soon as we had stated our conclusions the files were taken away again because they were top secret. That is why I introduced glasnost as soon as I became General Secretary of the Party. People knew nothing about what was going on in their country. But you can't transform a country if you withhold information from people. Nowadays, by contrast, everyone is in favour of conservation.

PARIS MATCH: And you, Nicolas Hulot, how did you become a conservationist?

N.H.: People all say they are in favour of conservation. Well and good, perhaps they are, in the depths of their soul. But the practical application of this knowledge is risibly inadequate. One comes to the conclusion, as you do, Mikhail Gorbachev, in your Manifesto, that humanity is somehow suffering a dose of autism. We are the victims of 'Titanic Syndrome': the orchestra continues playing while on every deck each individual is looking after his own interests. I wonder whether you were able to see all this clearly when you were in a position of power. Or is your clear view now in fact the result of your distance from power?

M.G.: No. In those years I did a great deal for environmental conservation. Once people had been given the possibility of speaking freely, the first meetings about ecology and the environment began to be held. Many adults and children were sick in 90 towns where chemical plants and other factories injurious to health were located. These meetings were so stormy that they could only be brought to a close by promising to solve the problem in the most heavily polluted towns. We closed down 1,300 factories, even large enterprises of which a number were unique. Some of them we modernised, but others remained closed for good. People have rights, they are sovereign.

PARIS MATCH: Mikhail Gorbachev, when one is head of state in the Kremlin and has to decide between closing down a factory or saving workplaces in order to avoid strikes and riots, isn't one forced to decide in favour of workplaces and against the environment? Or can one be a head of state who is in favour of ecology?

M.G.: The situation didn't allow for any choice. Some factories were closed down and others modernised. Of course that affected the economy and cost workplaces, but we found solutions. We were also occupied with the pollution of the Volga and its tributaries. Half the Russian population lives along the banks of the Volga (I have already written about this), so we called on 120 scientific institutes to investigate the problem; we developed a project, but unfortunately the collapse of the Soviet Union put an end to the finance.

N.H.: I want to try and see things on a global scale. Bussuet, a French philosopher, once said that people regret consequences but come to terms with causes. What is the cause of the destruction we are visiting on the earth — for example the conflict between human being and nature since the beginning of the industrial age? For a number of decades there have been only two types of society: collectivism on the one hand and capitalism on the other. And a study of the matter has shown us that both have failed.

M.G.: Yes indeed, you are quite right. But I didn't expect you to say that! Nature is destroyed as much by liberal as by socialist societies. The planned economy of a socialist society was aimed just as much at producing more. In capitalist societies profit was the aim, but the consequence was the same. I regard the consumer society as a disaster. We need a new economic model, and the most acceptable one is that of sustainable development in which the economy takes account of every social and ecological aspect. Unfortunately when people talk of new economies they mean new technologies, whereas what we ought to be talking about is an economy that conserves our biosphere. We human beings constitute the worst problem. As soon as the ecological organizations started to function people took to the streets and elected green parties to parliaments, and important things happened. Our task now is to strengthen this movement. Even during Green Cross's foundation meeting in 1992

— this was one of the most bitter discussions in Kyoto — we decided not to take upon ourselves the responsibilities of governments. But we have to make our contribution to the development of a global ecological awareness. That is why we worked out the Earth Charter with its ecological principles. It has met with enthusiasm in some countries; for example in Germany a third edition of 100,000 copies is being prepared. If citizens begin to think, then parliaments and governments will follow their example. So let us not stray from our chosen path.

Perhaps I shall break the rules of democracy, for if I am re-elected I shall stay in office as President of Green Cross International for a fourth term. I've been talking a lot about myself now, but do please tell us about your work and the aims it has achieved, Monsieur Hulot.

N.H.: It's our duty — especially if we have even a small amount of influence — to play a part in determining the course of history. The years in which we are now living are decisive in that it is still possible to reverse a number of trends. It is urgently necessary to redefine the word 'progress', to give it a new meaning and make it last. From the twentieth century we have inherited the technical, scientific, political, economic and intellectual tools. It is time to reorganize these in order to revert from being a merely materialistic society to being a society that possesses cultural and spiritual values. This may sound rather theoretical, but it is up to us to exert our influence on public opinion, on consumers and citizens and on leaders of public opinion. That is another reason why a world-wide organization needs to be created as a counterbalance to the World Trade Organization, for using the market as the only yardstick will lead humanity to a dead end.

PARIS MATCH: Mikhail Gorbachev, do you agree that there needs to be an independent organization like the one Nicolas Hulot is suggesting? Is it necessary to found a new organization, perhaps in Europe?

M.G.: Let me respond to Nicolas Hulot first and then I'll reply to your question. What is progress? Surely not merely achieving something better for ourselves. Progress should raise people who are no longer preoccupied solely with struggling to survive to a higher level, but at the same time it must also secure the conservation of nature and the harmony between man and nature. For me that is the most important criterion of progress. One of our poets, Andrei Vosnessenski, said that any progress was reactionary if human beings perished as a result of it; it was not worthwhile if it ruined nature and our earthly home. Progress ought to be defined as something that perfects the human being, that raises him up rather than being merely a matter of producing more motor cars. That would only call for everyone to start jogging to lose a lot of pounds!

N.H.: We often confuse progress with output.

M.G.: Nowadays, ten years on from unlimited globalization, new theoreticians are suggesting different criteria for progress. Of course some parts of the population are at an advantage as a result of this spontaneous globalization. The rich countries that have all the earth's wealth at their disposal maintain that sustainable development should be replaced by freedom in the market place. That is nonsense. And as for the creation of a new world-wide organization, there is already one that is recognized by UNESCO, namely Green Cross International.

N.H.: What is needed is an international authority as a counterpart to the UN.

M.G.: This is something one should certainly think about. The Marxists believed that you have to seize power because no one will give it to you! But I agree with you. On the other hand, all that is necessary is for enough people to join Green Cross International, for it is indeed a global organization. If enough persons of international stature were to join, we should be in a position to negotiate with international authorities.

PARIS MATCH: Do heads of state listen to you? Nicolas Hulot, you are an adviser to Jacques Chirac and are close to him. Mr Gorbachev, you are President of Green Cross International and direct your messages to President Bush. Does he listen to you?

M.G.: Once the question of disarmament and the destruction of chemical weapons came to the fore – and we possess sufficient chemical weapons to destroy the earth – I wrote to 35 heads of state, and they all replied. The Belgian, Swiss and British parliaments also invited me to come and initiate a debate. President Putin wrote that he understood my anxiety, and his budget for the destruction of chemical weapons has been increased sixfold. President Bush also replied, and there has been a debate in Congress.

PARIS MATCH: President Bush doesn't give an impression of listening very attentively when mention is made of the Kyoto Protocol . . .

M.G.: Well, it's not so simple. A few days ago I was talking to the American Secretary of State, Colin Powell, about environmental conservation. Congress has now given the President further powers in this matter. In 2002, 76 million dollars were earmarked for the creation of plants for the destruction of chemical weapons. We are in a trap of our own making. I also talked with Colin Powell about the Kyoto Protocol and told him that because of its economic strength America must take the lead. Or put the other way round, a leading power that plays a more important part and bears greater responsibility does not have the right to act as it likes. So we want to know why the United States and its current government are ignoring the Kyoto Protocol. Why has the USA frustrated the work of the World Commission on Water in the Netherlands, and why has it not ratified the Nuclear Threat Initiative? If the United States as a leading power behaves like this, what kind of example is this for other countries to follow? The American Secretary of State and I discussed these problems, and I believe that serious discussions are also taking place within the American government. Whatever the case may be, the Americans can no longer stay on the sidelines. Being a trained lawyer I am familiar with a saying we have: The law is like a telegraph pole; you can't climb over it but you can get round it. Well, ecology is not a law and we cannot get round it. We are up to our necks in trouble: resources are finite, the atmosphere is heavily polluted, so are the oceans . . .

PARIS MATCH: Jacques Chirac listens to you, Nicolas Hulot. But does he act?

N.H.: He certainly listens to me. But I have to be realistic, for as things stand practical implementation in France as well as in the other European countries is negligible. This is simply because few politicians have grasped the idea that sustainable development calls for a radical re-orientation . . .

M.G.: A transformation of Paradise.

N.H.: Exactly, so that it can at last be attained. Politicians have not yet realized that even if they are only partially abreast of the times but want to make decisions that take account of the future they could trigger a thorough revolution. For the factor of sustainable development will have to penetrate into all corners of society. Yet even politicians who have an economic plan and see things from a macro-economic perspective, and when they take account of the enormous environmental and health consequences – even then they still fail to comprehend that it is better to spend money in advance than afterwards, for example in the case of the annual floods here in France of which we humans are the cause.

M.G.: I agree entirely. We ourselves are responsible for the way nature has been unleashed in recent years.

N.H.: Although I cannot prove it scientifically, I am convinced that recent climatic anomalies are the first signs of climate change caused by the greenhouse effect. But to return to the attitude of certain American lobbies which, by the way, do not represent the whole of American public opinion . . .

M.G.: Quite right. Every year we hold meetings all over the United States and award prizes for important ecological contributions made by quite remarkable people.

N.H.: As I was saying, the attitude of certain lobbies is typical of a tragic turn of mind which presumes that technology and science will tomorrow solve the problems we are creating today. Such arrogance is guilty before history, for it denies help to our endangered planet. It is true that seen from the point of view of the threshold countries the attitude of the United States is dramatic in the way it fails to set an example.

But when you see a country like China announcing that it intends to sign the Kyoto Protocol . . .

M.G.: And Russia.

N.H.: . . . then I say to myself that this demonstrates nicely how the United States is becoming increasingly isolated. But to answer your question, Mikhail Gorbachev, as to what I am doing at my level, I have to say that unfortunately I have only words and writing to offer, although I too run a foundation. Of course it lacks the scope of your organization, but it does concern itself first and foremost with environmental education and supporting environmentally friendly projects.

M.G.: We have also started an ecological education programme for school children. Monsieur Hulot, I very much support what you have been saying: Countries that are incapable of solving their economic problems without damaging the environment and which do not practice disarmament are sick. It is not enough to fiddle about trying to cure a sick society when what is needed is a thoroughgoing reform.

P.M.: Is the pollution of the environment a form of terrorism?

M.G.: No, I wouldn't go as far as to say that. But terrorist attacks could of course have disastrous consequences for the environment, for example an attack on a nuclear installation or poisoning of the drinking water supply. We must fight terrorism in whatever way we can, for it is unjustifiable. It uses economic and social problems to recruit people who do not know any other way to go. It is an exceedingly dangerous phenomenon. Terrorism is unacceptable as a means of solving problems.

N.H.: Before 9/11 people more or less ignored the dangers of terrorism, at least on that scale. Humanity didn't want to admit how vulnerable it is. And to this day it ignores the fact that environmentally it is in just as much danger. What will have to happen before humanity realizes that the further it retreats from nature the more vulnerable it becomes?

M.G.: We ought also to think about the reasons why terrorists do what they do. They are people whose view of the world is psychologically abnormal. Think of the Red Brigades — their members were from rich families. Poverty is not necessarily the root of terrorism. Nevertheless, we shall have to regulate the flow of finance and fight against poverty in order to be able to defuse conflicts from which terrorism can emerge.

PARIS MATCH: Since 9/11 and in view of the threat of further terrorist attacks, is there a risk of environmental conservation being neglected?

M.G.: I don't think so. These are suspicions politicians have. Neither the struggle against poverty nor the measures in favour of ecology can be neglected. Terrorists speculate about poverty, and now politicians are also indulging in speculation . . .

N.H.: Nevertheless, there is a risk, though worries may sometimes be greater and sometimes less so. I hope very much indeed that the events of 9/11 will have made people realize one thing at least somewhat more clearly, namely that there is a part of humanity being excluded from hope and that even though this may have been just as much the case in former epochs, nowadays it is being done with a complete lack of decency.

M.G.: It's true that in the globalized world everything is different, not only global collaboration but also global terrorism.

N.H.: The one thing that has changed in our century is the fact that now people can no longer ignore one another. Those who shirk their responsibilities know very well that others are without hope, and those who are without hope know that those others are shirking their responsibilities. Such things become untenable at our present level of communication. That is what lies behind the suggestion which cannot be postponed, namely the introduction of a system of taxation that regulates financial markets, like the Tobin Tax. Economists maintain that it cannot be implemented, but I can't believe it to be impossible to work out a taxation mechanism aimed at currency transactions.

PARIS MATCH: Do you agree with a world-wide tax of this kind to maintain the earth?

M.G.: Most certainly. Within the framework of its globalization project the Gorbachev Foundation has been working for years on economic problems. We have produced a book which is being prepared for publication at the moment, and we have held a conference in Boston to remind the public about these matters. Three Nobel laureates, two of them economists, consider the Tobin Tax to be feasible. It would not have to be exactly that system, but something of the kind is definitely needed since huge funds must be found to solve the problems of providing potable water, to fight poverty and to support the education system in poor countries, so that new technologies can be created there.

PARIS MATCH: How many Chernobyls is the earth still threatened by?

M.G.: That depends on how we get on with doing our job.

PARIS MATCH: There is talk of 20 Chernobyls in the former Soviet Union. Can you confirm that number?

M.G.: No, I can't. I was talking about Chernobyl yesterday with a member of the Nobel Prize Commission. After all these years he considers the most plausible cause of the catastrophe to have been as follows: The director of the nuclear reactor had written a paper, and in order to confirm his hypothesis he had to experiment with the reactor core. Although operating instructions existed he changed them in order to carry out his experiments and thereby caused the explosion.

PARIS MATCH: Aren't you anxious about the risk of further Chernobyls in view of people's worries that so many badly equipped and badly planned nuclear plants exist?

M.G.: As you know, Russia has done a great deal to improve the safety of nuclear energy and the conditions for storing nuclear waste and chemical weapons. I have not been able to check on all this, but I rely on the word of the President who in his turn relies on reports from experts. Of course I know that such reports can also be less than adequate.

N.H.: I'm horrified to hear that the Chernobyl catastrophe is supposed to have been caused by the irresponsible experiments of a single person. That shows how vulnerable all these systems are and how necessary it is to set up independent elements of supervision and regulatory processes. But I ask myself whether humanity is not . . .

M.G.: A specific culture of work and responsibility is what is needed in such situations.

N.H.: . . . I ask myself whether humanity is not at this very moment engaged in an experiment on a global scale while playing the role of the sorcerer's apprentice . . .

M.G.: Or perhaps there is someone who is experimenting on us . . . But anyway, conservation of the environment is something that concerns us all.

Notes

By Galia Ackerman and Bernd Rullkötter

1 Namely the Russian Orthodox, the Greek Orthodox and the Armenian Orthodox churches.

2 Harvests were confiscated and given to the workers who were supposed to speed up the industrialization of the country; the measure also had the purpose of breaking any opposition to collectivization.

3 'Closed' towns and villages where armaments factories were located were frequently not even shown on maps. Foreigners were forbidden to enter them.

4 The meeting in December 1991 between Yeltsin, Kravchuk and Shushevich at Beloveshskaya Pushcha not far from Minsk ended with the declaration announcing the dissolution of the USSR.

5 Strategic Arms Reduction Talks which began at Geneva in 1982. The START 1 Agreement was signed in Moscow in 1991 and the START 2 Agreement in March 1993. However, the latter has to date not come into force although it was signed by the US Senate in 1996 and the Russian Duma in 2000. It cannot come into force until the US ratifies an Additional Protocol which Russia has already ratified.

6 Only a small group of officials authorized by the KGB could access these 'Special Archives' in the libraries.

7　In a referendum held in March 1991, 76 per cent of Soviet citizens voted in favour of retaining the Union state on the basis of absolute equality. However, the referendum only involved 11 of the 15 republics of the Union since the Baltic republics and Moldova had refused to participate.

8　In this new arms control agreement the US and Russia agreed to reduce their strategic nuclear arms within 10 years to an active stock of between 1,700 to 2,200 warheads each.

9　Organization for Economic Cooperation and Development founded in 1961. Its official aims are to coordinate economic policy and harmonize aid programmes of the developed nations. At present there are 30 member states.

10　This is how the French mass media described the fact that the candidate of the radical right-wing National Front, Jean-Marie Le Pen, entered the second round of the 2002 presidential election with the help of racist slogans.

11　Svetlana Alexiyevich, *Tschernobyl, Eine Chronik für die Zukunft* (Chernobyl, A chronicle for the future), Berlin 1997.

12　The Kyoto Protocol signed in 1997 obliges the industrialized nations to reduce their greenhouse gas emissions by an average of 5.2 per cent of the 1990 level by 2008–2012. The USA, which produces one fifth of the world's carbon dioxide emissions, was willing to reduce its emissions by as much as 7 per cent if the larger developing countries were also included in the programme. Since the developing countries in question rejected the proposal on the grounds that it would damage their economies, the American president, George W. Bush, refused to sign the Protocol.

13 Clive Ponting, *A Green History of the World: The Environment and the Collapse of Great Civilizations*, Harmondsworth 1992.

14 Edouard Le Roy, *L'exigence idéaliste et le fait d'évolution*, Paris 1927.

15 See the omnibus volume *Russki kosmism* (Russian Cosmism), Moscow 1993, which also includes the above-quoted work by Konstantin Tsiolkovski.

16 Jacques Attali, *Dictionnaire du XXI siècle*, Paris 1998.

17 Subsidies received by an American cotton grower amount to about $35,000, i.e. a third of his annual income.

18 This tax on international currency transactions was suggested in 1978 by the American economist James Tobin (1981 Nobel Prize for Economics) in order to limit speculation on the Stock Exchange. A measure of this kind would bring in 228 billion dollars annually which could be used to create conditions for long-term development in poorer countries.

19 Experts estimate this damage to amount to 1,300–1,500 billion dollars.

20 Pasko was arrested in November 1997 on suspicion of high treason and espionage. A court of the Pacific Fleet acquitted him in July 1999 but condemned him to a three-year prison sentence for abusing his position while at the same time granting him an amnesty. However, the Supreme Military Court decided to begin a new case against him in Vladivostok which led to a four-year sentence for high treason. This resulted in objections from around the world.

21 When this aerosol is inhaled it dissolves in the fluids of the lungs and bronchial tubes. Large amounts of radioactive par-

ticles are inhaled by anyone within a 300 metre radius of the spot where a grenade hits a tank. Although the level of radiation in the air is not high, an accumulation of radioactive particles in the human organism causes considerable damage, affecting organs, destroying chromosomes and reducing fertility. These consequences, which were observed among the international troops in Iraq and Kosovo and the civilian populations of Iraq and Yugoslavia, were also found to have affected the population in the contaminated zones around Chernobyl. People there were exposed to low-dose radiation over a long period by eating contaminated foods. The link between an accumulation of radioactive particles in the human organism and a number of diseases has been proven by Professor Yuri Bandashevski of Belarus.

22 The General Secretary of the Soviet Communist Party who was also the head of state was the only individual authorized to order a nuclear attack. For this reason he was permanently accompanied by officers carrying a case which contained the 'nuclear button' and a secret code.

23 India and North Korea also possess small stocks of chemical weapons. Old stocks of such weapons may also be buried in many European countries and also Japan.

24 A similar problem also arises in countries that have developed their nuclear energy economy rapidly. The cost of decommissioning old reactors and disposing of nuclear waste makes nuclear energy unprofitable in the long term.

25 Russian chemical weapons are simpler and therefore cost less to decommission.

26 Vladimir I. Vernadsky, *Der Mensch in der Biosphäre, Zur Naturgeschichte der Vernuft*, Frankfurt am Main 1997. (English edition: *Biosphere, Complete Annotated Edition*, New York 1998.)

27 Omnibus volume *Internationale iskusstva* (1919).

28 Stephen Jay Gould, *The Structure of Evolutionary Theory*, Harvard 2001.

29 Omnibus volume *Rossiya: Problemy ecologicheskoi bezopasnosti* (Russia: problems of ecological danger), ed. N. Kolikov, Moscow 1997.

30 The Earth Charter, Final Version, 24 March 2000. International Earth Charter Secretariat, c/o University for Peace, P.O.Box 319-6100, San José, Costa Rica; Phone: (506) 205-1600, Fax: (506) 249-3500, email: info@earthcharter.org, http://www.earthcharter.org

Unarmed Heroes
The Courage to go beyond Violence
Personal testimonies and essays on the peaceful resolution of conflict
Compiled and edited by peace direct

'...*An emotional journey where you can feel the heart and soul of the protagonist being poured out onto the page.... [Unarmed Heroes] gives us the opportunity to gather our thoughts and start to take action.... I can see this book becoming one of the milestones in the creation of a strong, articulate and powerful peace constituency.*' – Dame Anita Roddick, founder, The Body Shop

In any war there are always people who, rather than pick up an AK 47, will take the difficult route of active peacemaking. There are individuals in the midst of the violence in Afghanistan, Northern Ireland, even in the D.R. Congo, who are risking their lives to prevent other people getting killed. This book tells their stories. Featuring sixteen personal testimonies by those who have summoned up the courage to transform violence in their lives, *Unarmed Heroes* is an inspiration as well as a handbook for overcoming conflict. The contributors, drawn from all over the globe, include relatives of those who died in the World Trade Centre attack and the Oklahoma bombing; Israeli, Palestinian and Afghan peace activists; a former IRA bomber and the daughter of one of his victims; a British military commander turned anti-nuclear campaigner, and many others. Despite their diverse backgrounds, each shares a passion for working actively but peacefully for positive change.

Such stories might leave us in awe, doubting our own ability to emulate these brave examples. But this book features an accessible DIY section which shows, step-by-step, how anyone can take constructive steps to change their own life and learn the skills of resolving conflict. It also includes a comprehensive Resources section.

Unarmed Heroes is essential reading: an invaluable tool for the growing global movement of people determined to challenge violent responses to international, regional, local and family conflicts.

272pp; 21.5 × 13.5 cm; paperback; £10.95; ISBN 1 902636 52 X

The Party's Over
Oil, War and the Fate of Industrial Societies
Richard Heinberg

'*If societies a century from now have managed to learn how to live peacefully, modestly, and sustainably, it may be at least partly because the advice in this timely book was heeded.*' — Thom Hartmann, author of *The Last Hours of Ancient Sunlight*

Without oil, what would you do? How would you travel? How would you eat? What would everyday life be like?

The world is about to change dramatically and permenantly as a result of oil depletion. Within the next few years, the global production of oil will peak. Thereafter, even with a switch to alternative energy sources, industrial societies will have less energy available to do all the things essential to their survival. We are entering a new era as different from the industrial one as the latter was from mediaeval times.

The Party's Over deals head-on with the imminent decline of cheap oil. It shows how oil and war have been closely related for the past century, and how competition to control oil supplies is likely to lead to new resource wars in the Middle East, Central Asia, and South America. Tracing the crucial role of fossil fuels in the rise of industrialism, Heinberg discusses the degree to which energy alternatives can compensate for oil, and recommends:

- a managed transition to a slower-paced, low-energy, sustainable society in the future;
- a global programme of resource conservation and sharing implemented by the US — the world's foremost oil consumer and the most mightily armed nation in world history — in concert with other countries; and
- realistic ways for families, communities, nations, and the world to prepare for the coming crisis.

A riveting wake-up call that does for oil depletion what Rachel Carson's *Silent Spring* did for the issue of chemical pollution — i.e. raising to consciousness a previously ignored global problem of immense proportions—*The Party's Over* is essential reading for all those concerned with the future of modern life as we know it.

Updated and revised edition; 320pp; 23.5 × 15.5 cm; paperback; £12.99; ISBN 1 905570 00 7

Powerdown
Options and Actions for a Post-Carbon World
Richard Heinberg

Resource depletion and population pressures are about to catch up with us, and no one is prepared. Oil is running out and, if the Western world continues with its current policies, the next decades will likely be marked by war, economic collapse, and environmental catastrophe. The political élites, especially in the US, have shown themselves to be unwilling to deal with the situation, and have in mind a punishing game of 'Last One Standing'.

There are alternatives. A 'Powerdown' strategy, for example, would aim to reduce per-capita resource usage in wealthy countries, develop alternative energy sources, distribute resources more equitably, and reduce the human population humanely but systematically over time. It could save us, but will require tremendous effort and economic sacrifice.

Powerdown speaks frankly to these dilemmas. Avoiding cynicism and despair, it begins with an overview of the likely impacts of oil and natural gas depletion and then outlines four options for industrial societies during the next decades:

- **Last One Standing**: the path of competition for remaining resources;
- **Powerdown**: the path of cooperation, conservation, and sharing;
- **Waiting for a Magic Elixir**: wishful thinking, false hopes, and denial;
- **Building Lifeboats**: the path of community solidarity and preservation.

Finally, the book explores how three important groups within global society – the power élites, the organized opposition to the élites (the 'activist' movements), and ordinary people – are likely to respond to these four options. Timely, accessible and eloquent, *Powerdown* is clarion call to urgent action.

224pp; 23.5 × 15.5 cm; paperback; £10.95; ISBN 1 902636 63 5

For a full catalogue contact:

Clairview Books
Hillside House
The Square
Forest Row
RH18 5ES
UK

office@clairviewbooks.com

www.clairviewbooks.com